Applied Linguistics and Language Study

GENERAL EDITOR: C. N. CANDLIN

Linguistic Theory, Linguistic Description and Language Teaching

EDDY ROULET

Translation by Christopher N. Candlin

LONGMAN

LONGMAN GROUP LIMITED
London

*Associated companies branches and
representatives throughout the world*

© AIMAV (Association internationale
pour la recherche et la diffusion des
méthodes audio-visuelles et structuro-
globales) 1972

English Translation © Longman Group
Limited 1975

This edition first published by Longman
Group Limited 1975
Second impression 1976
Third impression 1979

ISBN 0 582 55075 0

Text set in 10/12 pt Monotype Times
New Roman, printed in Great Britain
by Lowe & Brydone Printers Limited,
Thetford, Norfolk.

Contents

Preface

Two viewpoints present themselves in attempts to define the scope and subject matter of Applied Linguistics: either, in an attempt to define the bases for syllabuses and learning materials, one examines the current state of linguistic theory and sets about proposing illustrated restatements of existing formal descriptions premissed on one such theory, or one embarks from particular problems of explanation and learning thrown up in the process of materials construction, syllabus design or language instruction, and seeks for clarification and potential explanatory value from a range of such formal descriptions leavened by psycholinguistic experimentation.

If one adopts the former approach, and in its narrow sectarian form, a trap quickly opens of evaluating syllabuses and materials according to criteria which are more appropriate to evaluating competing linguistic theories. As Professor Roulet accurately points out, language teachers and syllabus designers are then blown in a variety of directions by shifts in the theoretical wind. If for no other reason, the lack of any necessary isomorphism between linguistic categories and units and language learning categories and units would seem to make this naive view of 'applying linguistics' untenable.

If, on the other hand, one adopts the second, classroom and problem-centred approach, one can easily capsize in the attractive delights of eclecticism. Avoiding the God's Truth approach of, say, cartooning structural linguistics or clinging to the Grammar of Case compels the teacher and syllabus designer into a hocus-pocus search for a pedagogical grammar which will successfully mediate and interpret between formal grammars and the problems thrown up by the classroom. The task for such a pedagogical grammar will be less one of measuring up to the adequacy criteria encumbent on formal grammars, but rather of making a principled choice between their offerings and explanations in the light of specific learning problems of particular audiences.

Whether, however, one adopts the first or the second approach, awareness of the applied potential of formal descriptions and the theoretical premises upon which they are constructed is indispensable for the teacher and syllabus designer. It is in this area of 'awareness of potential' that Professor Roulet's contribution to the *Applied Linguistics and Language Study Series* is most valuable.

In this area, the book devotes considerable space to competing theories: in a readable commentary on central issues, the contribution of structural linguistics as an objective alternative to the fictions and misconceived formulations of traditional school grammars is explored, and in his portrayal of the accepted theoretical and descriptive critiques of generative linguistics to structuralism, Roulet does not fall into the strident trap of assuming that because major *theoretical* objections to structuralism can be raised this necessarily invalidates structural descriptions entirely for language teaching and *applied* purposes. It is in such issues that the author's applied linguistic experience serves him well in mitigating what, in others, is frequently a theoretical stance.

From this critical historical analysis the author is equipped to take the reader to a treatment of the current question in applied linguistics: that if a pedagogical grammar is to be at the basis of language teaching materials, if such materials have as their aim to lead the learner to knowledge of the target language, then both they and the pedagogical grammar must be concerned with the rules of language *use* as they are with the rules of grammaticality and the well-formedness of sentences. In a section specially written for the English translation, Professor Roulet takes up this question of the components of communicative competence and argues, once more from the standpoint of the problem-centred approach, that our awareness of the potential of linguistic theory and linguistic descriptions for language teaching materials and syllabuses must include the pragmatic requirement of a centre on semantics and the sociopsychology of discourse.

Christopher N. Candlin,
General Editor,
Applied Linguistics and Language Study

to Cécile

Introduction

The problem of applying linguistic theory and linguistic description to modern language teaching is a central concern of linguists and teachers. Sol Saporta noted in 1966: 'A central question in the application of linguistics to the teaching of foreign languages involves the conversion of a scientific grammar into a pedagogical grammar'.[1]

Applied linguists are clear that their discipline cannot be content with deriving information solely from general linguistics or from descriptive linguistics, and that it needs to rely on other disciplines as, for example, psycholinguistics (for the study of learning strategies) or sociolinguistics (for the definition of teaching aims). In addition, they realize the need to redefine the role of linguistic theory and linguistic description amid all the other disciplines which might be able to contribute to renewing and improving language teaching methods.[2] This realization is most apparent in the central and very controversial domain of grammar, where the same kind of questions continually recur: what ought to be the place in the setting out of the content and gradation of a language course of information provided by linguistic theory and linguistic description? What kind of grammar are we to teach?[3] The problem becomes all the more important when one takes into account the fact that the information provided by linguistic theory and linguistic description not only concerns traditional instruction in grammar and spelling, but all the areas of language learning; performance in writing (composition), understanding material read, oral performance and comprehension and the stylistic study of literary texts, etc., all of which areas considerably enlarge the field of applications. Language teachers, for their part, have abruptly found themselves in a new situation; namely the condemnation of traditional grammar and the proliferation of new grammars for which they have not been prepared. This is partly due to the fact that up until the beginning of the twentieth century, linguistic theory, linguistic description and language teaching were considered as one entity; the Port-Royal Grammar[4] is an excellent example. For language teachers as for the public at large there was only a single grammar of French or English, the model for which had been placed somewhere in heaven and from which teachers had only to derive teaching grammars by simplifying and summarizing their exposition while giving out hints and in appending exemplificatory exercises to the stated rules. As a result, writers invested all their effort in devising new ways in which the coursebooks could be presented; choice of terminology, examples, introduction of explanatory and re-capitulative tables, the use of colours, illustrations, etc., without, how-ever, modifying the content and without posing to themselves from the outset the problem of the validity of the underlying grammatical description. An example of this tradition, which is still very much alive, is the publication of Malzac's: *Grammaire nouvelle du français*[5] which in a radically new form, i.e. in terms of a programmed course, nonetheless reproduces the content of traditional coursebooks. The only advantage of this essentially conservative and repetitive system was that the teacher could content himself in his teaching with gram-matical formulations which he had himself received in his own schooling.

The rapid development of linguistic studies in the nineteenth century, in particular in Germany, did little to change matters; comparative linguists were concerned particularly with the study of ancient lan-guages and were interested in the area of linguistic evolution and the genetic relationships between languages which had little to do with the interests of language teachers. It was in the twentieth century with the publication of the works of de Saussure, Palmer and Bloom-field,[6] that a general and descriptive science of linguistics was estab-lished which succeeded in overturning traditional grammar and radically modifying our conception of the system and function of language. Although these early studies were especially concerned with the analysis of phonological systems, work on grammatical analysis has predominated since the 1940s, but, anticipating the later necessary and predictable development of more complex research into semantic analysis, the last thirty years have seen the development of at least ten or more models of grammatical analysis which are of general interest and which have already been applied to the description of a number of languages. In America, for example, Wells' Immediate Constituent Analysis,[7] Harris' Distribution Analysis,[8] Pike's Tagmemic Grammar,[9] Lamb's Stratificational Grammar,[10] Chomsky's Transformational Generative Grammar[11] and Fillmore's Case Grammar[12] have been developed; and, similarly in Europe, Weisgerber's Content Grammar,[13] Martinet's Functional Syntax,[14] Tesnière's Dependency Grammar[15] and Halliday's Scale and Category Grammar.[16] It follows from such a list that there is no longer a single grammar of contemporary English or contemporary French, but numerous descriptions which often reflect very different conceptions of the system of language and of the strategies of language acquisition. Consequently, language teachers, becoming more and more aware of the gaps in traditional manuals, were no longer able to evade the question of what grammar to teach. Furthermore, certain models like Transformational Generative Grammar resorted to such abstract, complex and formal descriptions that teachers asked themselves with some justification how desirable, let alone possible it was for them to apply such recent models of grammar to the teaching of modern languages. Thus, despite the urgent need for co-operation, it appears as if a gulf is widening today between the work of linguists and the practical problems of language teachers. Frustrated by linguistic theories and grammatical descriptions which their inadequate linguistic training prevents them from understanding and evaluating, and irritated by the advice of general linguists or, indeed, applied linguists who often are unaware of pedagogical theory and practice, language teachers end up by losing all interest in the problem and retire within themselves, content with their experience and their prescriptions for teaching practice borrowed from this or that source.

This cannot be a satisfactory solution. Present controversy and vacillation on the application of linguistics to language teaching ought to serve in no way as an alibi for the return to traditional teaching or the elaboration of a simple collection of prescriptions for the utilization of audio-visual techniques as is all too often maintained today. G. Helbig makes the issue quite clear; 'It is not only a question today of modernizing the teaching of foreign languages by the use of language laboratories and audio-visual methods but also of obtaining through a clear understanding of modern linguistics much deeper insights into the system and function of language. This is the only way of assuring the success of language teaching in the long run.'[17]

There is no doubt that recent linguistic theories and grammatical descriptions have an important contribution to make to the modernizing of language teaching but at the same time it has to be admitted that the relationships between linguistic theory, the linguistic description of a single language, and a language teaching course are not as simple or as direct as one has in recent years perhaps too often thought them to be. As Wardhaugh points out: 'Too often in the past, the assumption has been made that linguistic technique could be made into a pedagogical technique or that apparent insights into linguistic structure achieved by linguists should be communicated rather directly to learners'.[18] The explanation of the relationships which hold between linguistic theory, the description of a single language and language teaching itself constitutes one of the central problems of applied linguistics in its concern with language teaching.

This book does not claim to put forward an established model for these relationships; we are not yet equipped with all the necessary components for such a model, in particular in the areas of language acquisition and language use. What can be proposed while referring as precisely and as often as possible to source materials, is an indication of representative ideas and most current applications; i.e.:

(1) A recapitulation of the principal shortcomings which justified a reformation of traditional school grammars.

(2) An indication of what it is that structural and transformational generative grammars can bring to the description and teaching of modern languages and a submission of this contribution to critical examination.

(3) An attempt at distinguishing the varied notions and ideas masked by the label 'Application of a Grammatical Model to Language Teaching', by reference to the debates and controversies of the last twenty years.

(4) An attempt to define the role of linguistic theory and linguistic description and more generally of linguistics as a whole, among those disciplines which have been called upon to contribute to an updating of language teaching methods.

NOTES

1 'Applied Linguistics and Generative Grammar' p. 81.

2 cf. Pit Corder: *Applied Linguistics: Various Interpretations and Practices* 1971.

3 cf. G. Nickel: 'Welche Grammatik für den Fremdsprachenunterricht?' and J. C. Chevalier: 'Quelle grammaire enseigner?'.

4 Arnault and Lancelot: *Grammaire générale et raisonnée*.

5 cf. the review by C. Müller in *Bulletin CILA*, 14, 1971 pp. 54–58.

6 F. de Saussure: *Course in General Linguistics* 1916 (trans W. Baskin). H. E. Palmer: *The Scientific Study and Teaching of Languages* 1917. L. Bloomfield: *Language* 1933.

7 R. Wells: 'Immediate Constituents' 1947.

8 Z. S. Harris: *Methods in Structural Linguistics* 1951.

9 K. L. Pike: *Language in relation to a Unified Theory of the Structure of Human Behaviour* 1954–1960.

10 S. Lamb: *An Outline of Stratificational Grammar* 1966.

11 N. Chomsky: *Syntactic Structures* 1957. *Aspects of the Theory of Syntax* 1965.

12 C. J. Fillmore: 'The Case for Case' 1968.

13 L. Weisgerber: *Grundzüge der inhaltsbezogenen Grammatik*.

14 A. Martinet: *Eléments de linguistique générale* 1960.

15 L. Tesnière: *Eléments de syntaxe structurale* 1959. H. J. Heringer: 'Einige Ergebnisse und Probleme der Dependenzgrammatik' 1970.

16 M. A. K. Halliday: 'Categories of the Theory of Grammar' 1961.

17 G. Helbig: 'Zur Anwendbarkeit moderner linguistischer Theorien im Fremdsprachenunterricht und zu den Beziehungen zwischen Sprach- und Lerntheorien' p. 290.

18 R. Wardhaugh: 'Some reflections on the state of the art' p. 11.

1

Traditional Grammar

No doubt one can find as many traditional grammars as there are traditional grammarians and traditional manuals. Nevertheless, manuals of school grammar all fall into a certain number of characteristic errors which have often been pointed out by linguists[1] and can be usefully recalled at this point. This does not simply, however, totally rejecting traditional grammar as did the structuralists. In his book *Cartesian Linguistics*, Chomsky has shown pertinently that certain traditional works, for example the Port-Royal Grammar, presented a description of grammatical facts more accurate and more complete than that of a number of so-called structural grammars. Lyons, in his excellent *Introduction to Theoretical Linguistics* gives a timely reminder of the richness and delicacy of traditional analysis while pointing out that these are qualities which have been about for a long time in the majority of school grammar books.

Having once made this clear, however, it is still necessary to make the point that an examination of traditional school grammars indicates that they act as useful aids neither to the mastery of oral expression nor to that of written expression; both important objectives of modern language teaching. As to mastering oral and written comprehension, one might have been able to say more about that if it had ever been considered as an integral part of traditional teaching. In fact, the implicit aim of traditional school grammars, teaching the pupil to construct correct sentences, could not be achieved because of the nature of the *content* of these grammars and their manner of *presentation*[2] of grammatical data. Beginning with *content*, there are six major gaps (among others) which are characteristic of the majority of school grammars and which are damaging to modern language teaching practice:

(1) *Traditional manuals take no account of present-day language usage* and impose norms generally derived from the language of the great authors of previous centuries.

5

J. C. Chevalier writes: 'Too many grammars are still full of all kinds of expressions which nobody or practically nobody uses any longer, while, on the contrary, paying no attention to frequent colloquial usage.'[3] Like the teacher, the grammarian sets himself up as a legislator and adopts prescriptive attitudes. It is very natural that in order to support his authority, he should refer to the great authors of the past. To be clear on this point, it is enough to look at a work which, although it was not written for this particular goal, is still frequently used for the teaching of French to foreigners: Grévisse's *Précis de grammaire française*. A rapid run through this work shows that a third of the examples are made up of quotations from great authors, half of which are 17th Century writers. We could accept this if it were simply a matter of extracts from prose texts, where the examples in question show a number of points in common with contemporary French, but a hundred or so of the examples are taken from the poetry of La Fontaine and Racine as for example:

'Moi, qui, grâce aux dieux, de courage me pique, En ai pris la fuite de peur', which can hardly be considered as representative of present-day language usage. Further, is it necessary to fall back on the authority of Molière:

'Aucun juge par vous ne sera visité?'[5] to justify the usage of *aucun* if in presenting it to the student you do not warn him of a use of the interrogative which is not current today?

Whatever interests a certain category of students may have in classical or poetic language, the grammarian ought first to describe the language in current use; it is that language which the students rely on for daily communication. As an example, traditional manuals for the most part omit constructions current in contemporary French, in particular in the area of interrogative constructions. If we take the nuclear interrogation with *où, quand, pourquoi, comment, combien* as an example, Grévisse seems to admit constructions of the type *où va-t-il?, où va ton père?, où ton père va-t-il?*[6], and as an *emphatic* form *où est-ce que tu vas?*[7] The intuition of present-day speakers of French would not accord this last form any more emphasis or insistence than the others. Furthermore, the researches of the *Français Fondamental*[8] group have shown that the above four forms make up only a little more than half of the forms currently in use in the fifties: the following is a summary (the numbers refer to the five morphemes mentioned above):

où va ton père?	134	
où va-t-il?		168 forms allowed
où ton père va-t-il?	4	by Grévisse
où est-ce qu'il va?	30	
il va où?	45	
où il va?	77	139 forms
où c'est qu'il va?	12	excluded
où qu'il va?	5	

These figures plainly show that this particular manual is treating a language which is not at all representative of the spoken French of the fifties (without mentioning the language of the sixties which would doubtless provide even more surprising figures!) It is not the suggestion that it is necessary to teach the use of all these forms in class but since pupils will have to hear them and understand them sooner or later, perhaps it is better to avoid unpleasant surprises by presenting them with the facts. This is more especially true since there are worse consequences of a too normative teaching method: pupils rapidly realize that there is a divorce between the language they study in class and the language they spontaneously use as a mother tongue or hear around them as a second language. At this point they rapidly lose interest in learning grammar.

(2) *Even the most recent traditional manuals only describe the written language and either take no account of the spoken language or mix the two codes.* Take the following rule, presented in an English coursebook very much in use in Swiss and French schools and which appears very modern (illustrations, phonetic transcriptions, substitution tables, etc.):

'The majority of words form their plural by adding an 's' which is pronounced. For example: a boy, two boys [bɔiz]'.[9] Notice that this example in fact contradicts the rule—the *s* of *boys* is not pronounced as [s]—and although the authors mention further on plurals in -*es* and -*ies* in the written language, they do not treat the distribution of the forms [s], [z] and [iz] in spoken language. Similar remarks hold true for the rules for the formation of the third person singular of the Simple Past.

1. The regular simple past is formed by adding *ed* to the infinitive stem, e.g. (call) called, (open) opened.

2. When the infinitive stem of the verb ends in *e* you add a *d*, e.g. (smile) smiled.

3. For monosyllabic verbs ending in a single consonant preceded by a single vowel, you double the final consonant before adding *ed*, e.g. (stop) stopped, (clap) clapped.[10]

Thus, we have a good many observations on the forms of the written language but no allusions to the nature and distribution of the spoken language forms [d], [t], [id] although very different from those of the written language. In the same way, no account is taken of the fact that forms taught as special or exceptional cases in written language are perfectly regular in the spoken language; [kaeriz] is formed on the same model as [pleiz], and [rʌbd] on the same model as [kɔːld] even though *carries* is a special case in the written code (ending -*ies*) as is *rubbed* (doubling of the final consonant).

In speaking of manuals for the teaching of French, E. Wagner notes, perfectly correctly, that these courses 'aimed at both Frenchmen and foreign learners begin from a hypothesis which is constantly present, if not formulated, namely, that the linguistic activity of the speaker remains the same whether it is a question of using the spoken language or the written. Differences of use, whether in the lexicon or in the grammar or in the phonology are passed over in silence or minimised'.[11] Modern linguistic research has exhaustively shown that the spoken language is organized into a system which, to a remarkable extent, is different from the system of the written language. This is particularly striking in French and in English. Csecsy has demonstrated this in his study of the morphology of the French verb[12] and Dubois, after comparing gender and number forms in spoken and written French and their distribution says that: 'A systematic and parallel study of equivalent utterances in the spoken and written code makes quite clear the dissymmetry of the two systems and their relatively autonomous function'.[13] Grammars which distinguish the two codes are quite rare and course books which do so as, for example, Mauger,[14] do not manage to avoid confusion. As an example, the following is the general rule given for the formation of the feminine of nouns.

'In writing, an *e* is added to the masculine singular; in spoken French, consonants which are thus rendered intervocalic are pronounced:

—ais: un Anglais, une Anglaise
—ain: un châtelain, une châtelaine etc'.[15]

Notice here that the examples are solely concerned with the written language and the rule given for the spoken language is incomplete in that it fails to refer to the existence of denasalization.

If one admits that the structures of the spoken language are quite different from those of the written language and that traditional manuals systematically present only the structures of the written language, at best, or produce a confusion between the two codes, and if one acknowledges that teachers in general do not have the two codes, and if one acknowledges that teachers in general do not have an explicit satisfactory knowledge of the spoken language, one is driven to the conclusion that the information provided by traditional grammars cannot enable pupils to attain one of the fundamental objectives of modern language learning, the acquisition of a mechanism for oral communication.

(3) *Traditional coursebooks devote a great deal of time to secondary grammatical points (in particular orthography) but pay little attention to important constructions.* In this way, Grévisse's *Précis* which runs to three hundred pages, devotes three pages to nouns with double gender (pp. 64–67), seven to the words *tout, même* and *quelque* (pp. 108–114) and twelve to participial agreement (208–219) but does not treat the structure of different types of noun phrase at all. Each of the constituents of the phrases: *tous les petits enfants noirs, le jour le plus long, un tout petit animal blessé*, is presented from the point of view of its semantics and morphology in one or other chapters of the work, but the foreign student will not be able to find rules for combining these elements anywhere so as to allow him to produce the noun phrases in question. This is because traditional coursebooks in general prefer to teach the student how to avoid the most common exceptions to the norm rather than lead him to construct utterances. 'The student studies all those things which he ought to avoid but he doesn't learn what he ought to do' as L. F. and A. P. Nilsen pertinently note.[16]

(4) *More generally, traditional coursebooks give a predominant place to morphology, and neglect syntax.* To justify this comment it is only necessary to point out the part accorded in grammars of French to the morphology of nouns and adjectives where authors usually set out exhaustive lists of all the idiosyncratic cases (adjectives which only apply to feminine nouns: *cochère, dire, grège, pie, poulinière, suitée, théologale, trémière, vomique,* or to masculines: *aquilin, pers, saur,* etc.),[17] while the use of the pronoun *en,* albeit very complex,[18] is dismissed in a page and a half.[19] The same is true when one looks at the chapter on the verb, where a large section of it (forty pages in Grévisse and in Mauger) is given over to morphology. As a result, syntactic information on the organization of the verb phrase, of extreme importance to the construction of utterances, is simply absent. Since this information is also not generally to be found in dictionaries, foreign

learners of French are left to themselves. Grévisse[20] and Mauger[21] hardly treat at all a process as interesting and productive as that of causative transformations in French which permit the formation of one phrase from another by the introduction of a new agent as in:

les enfants mangent la soupe→la bonne fait [les enfants mangent la soupe]→la bonne fait manger la soupe aux enfants
la sécrétaire envoie une convocation à tous les membres→le directeur a fait [la sécrétaire envoie une convocation à tous les membres] →le directeur a fait envoyer une convocation à tous les membres par la sécrétaire.
les enfants sont tristes→la pluie fait [les enfants sont tristes]→la pluie rend les enfants tristes.[22]

Only the *Grammaire Larousse du français contemporain* devotes two pages to it (pp. 326–327) but without presenting any systematic rules. It is obviously more important for communication to know how to construct an utterance than to know how to put together all its constituents correctly in their variant combinations.

(5) *A corollary of this is where traditional grammars do not set out rules enabling the learner to construct systematically correct complex sentences.* All types of main and dependent clauses are set out clearly through the grammars but what are absent are the rules permitting the combination of several clauses for the construction of more and more complex structures. In this area the pupil, or more seriously the teacher, is left entirely to himself. If the teaching of written expression continues to be left to chance and uncertain methods, this is in large measure due to the weakness of manuals of traditional grammar.

(6) *Finally, outside the area of morphology and syntax, the treatment of lexis and phonology is very often inadequate.* Thus Grévisse presents the sounds of French from a strictly *phonetic*[23] point of view despite the fact that it is the phonological system which is of greatest interest for the pupil studying his mother tongue and of the most use for those who study it as a foreign language. Furthermore, Grévisse takes no account of those highly important phenomena for the learning of French as a foreign language, e.g. the use of schwa, and vocalic and consonantal liaison.[24] In short, the information he does provide cannot in any way be seen to support the systematic teaching of pronunciation and reading. As to the presentation of lexical sets, homonyms, paronyms, synonyms and antonyms,[25] this is too frequently too elementary and takes no account at all of syntagmatic

relations or collocational relations, the importance of which Galisson has shown for the learning of vocabulary.[26]

If these are important gaps in the content of such works, they are even more serious in the lay-out or presentation of the grammar.

1. *Traditional grammars present definitions, rules and explanations very frequently of a logicosemantic character which are insufficiently explicit, often false and therefore both dangerous and of little value.* As an example, in one of the most recent grammars to appear the author gives the following definition:

> 'A sentence is a more or less complex expression offering the complete sense of a thought, feeling or wish'.[27]

This is a definition so vague that it would apply perfectly adequately to a word, to a sentence, to a paragraph, to a chapter or indeed to a book; it is of little value as a definition and does not allow the student to grasp what a sentence is if he did not already intuitively know it. What use is there in talking about complexity in imprecise terms like 'more or less'? This feature does not in any way describe the nature of the complex sentence. How is one to define a complete sense; and a thought, a feeling, a wish? A hundred informants would produce a hundred different definitions of these terms. If you were then to add them up you would produce just as many definitions of the sentence. As a further example the same publication gives a definition of the direct object:

> 'The *object* of the verb is the term indicating the being or the object acted upon'. [28]

Such a definition is still false because it would apply equally easily to the subjects of sentences: *Jean a reçu une gifle* and *Jean a été renversé par une voiture.* One could cite a large number of examples to provide evidence for the weakness of traditional grammars on this point; one would then see just how many rules, definitions and explanations are either confusing or incomprehensible. Given then that numerous items of grammatical information are not set out explicitly by the author, it appears to teachers and pupils that they must derive the rules for themselves from the few examples which are given them. What follows is that the more teachers and pupils you have, the more different interpretations you have and as a result the more possible errors you have. K. Schap presents a similar criticism of the rules proposed by traditional grammar for the teaching of composition:

'Although the traditionalist may have good intuitions about his language, his grammar only enables him to make invulnerable statements about language; and since his statements are not subject to empirical proof, any statement he makes about teaching composition must take the form of an ad hoc rule. The rule about using pronouns in paragraphs provides a good example of the kind of statement the traditionalist can make. While this rule is apparently true, the vocabulary available to the traditionalist does not enable the kind of explanation which the student wants and needs.'[29]

2. *Traditional grammars present definitions and explanations which are often incoherent because they refer to a range of quite heterogeneous criteria.* Parts of speech provide an excellent example: Grévisse[30] and Schaap[31] for French and English, have recourse occasionally to functional criteria (adjectives) occasionally to formal criteria (prepositions) and occasionally to an amalgam of several criteria to the point that one does not know which category is being applied to which term. *Vol* is neither a being nor a thing nor an idea;[32] on the other hand, the term expresses an action[33] and is therefore presumably a verb? Why is the interrogative *qui* a pronoun when the *où* in the interrogative is always an adverb?[34] One begins to understand the confusion among the pupils.

3. *Traditional grammars give grammatical information in a compartmentalized and diffuse manner.* The way the chapters are laid out according to parts of speech is a good example of this: articles, nouns, adjectives, pronouns, verbs, adverbs, prepositions, conjunctions, interjections. What results from this is a very strange progression through the language. In a grammar of French intended for foreign students,[35] one begins by studying twenty cases of article usage (pp. 7–19) then the feminine and plural of nouns and adjectives, (pp. 19–41), then different adjectives and pronouns, only reaching the verb as the central item in the construction of verb phrase at page 84! Another difficulty inherent in this mode of presentation is the scattering through the grammar of information which relates to the same problem. In Grévisse's *Précis*, any pupil or teacher searching for information on the constructions of interrogatives in French has great difficulty since the information is scattered over pages 50, 106, 135, 176 and 230, and even then he still will not be in a position to find all the necessary information on these constructions. Finally, a major inconvenience is the way in which information is compartmentalized. The traditional distinction drawn between articles, possessive adjectives and demonstrative adjectives has hidden from the eyes of the grammarian and equally from the eyes of the teacher

and pupil, the way in which the system of predeterminers and determiners operates in modern French. This has been pointed out very clearly by Mitterand and Chevalier.[36] 'Each of the series', writes Mitterand, 'is defined by its semantic content (demonstratives, possessives, etc.) and studied in its alphabetical position, i.e. in a completely disorganized fashion as far as linguistics is concerned.'[37]

4. *In the way in which the data is presented, traditional grammar still follows too closely the grammatical systems of Greek and Latin which are not appropriate for the description of modern languages.* Clearly, one no longer declines:

father	(nominative)
o father	(vocative)
father	(accusative)
of the father	(genitive)
to, by or from the father	(dative)

but one still finds a chapter in a grammar of English in 1960 which is given over to the treatment of case—nominative, vocative, genitive, accusative, dative,[38] that is to say case endings which have more or less disappeared in modern English.

5. *In keeping with their normative aims, another major fault in traditional grammars is a tendency to accord an exaggerated importance to faults to be avoided by the learner and to exceptions. In so doing they frequently fail to reveal the systematic aspect of language.* Peytard and Genouvrier make the point exactly: 'the normative tradition thus led to excesses; to an atomistic grammar where essential facts, if picked up at all, were lost among incidentals. This led both to serious errors as much as to a frequently ineffective teaching methodology, very often away from the realities of the contemporary language, the precise needs of the students'.[39] In according an unwarranted place to the plural of nouns or to the agreement of past participles; in concentrating on the classification of rules and exceptions, school grammars emphasize the prescriptive and mechanical, rather than the systematic aspect of grammar, which is of great concern to present-day linguistic research. In fact, they actively discourage pupils' capacities for observation and analysis. As a result both teacher and pupils cease to have any interest in grammar, regard it as a burden and fall back on literature, the only area where they are permitted to exercise their intuitions, their observation and their creative talent.

6. *Although one commonly associates traditional grammars with the idea of the rule, a detailed examination shows that these grammars, on a*

number of important points, give fewer rules than they do lists of forms and examples. As Chomsky writes: 'the most careful and compendious traditional grammar may give a full account of exceptions and irregularities but it provides only examples and paradigmatic instances of regular constructions, together with various informal hints and remarks as to how the reader is to generalize from these instances. The basic regular processes of sentence construction remain unexpressed. It is the task of the reader to infer them from the presented material, it turns out that to fill this gap is no small task'.[40] Thus one is aware today of the importance of regular nominalization rules in the construction of the sentence,[41] yet the recent grammars of French which we have cited still content themselves with giving lists of suffixes which are of little value.[42] They do not provide any specific rule.

7. *A further important fault with traditional grammars is that the rules are not ordered in any way.* As a result they do not provide the teacher with any information on the progression he is to follow in his course, and to the pupil they give no assistance on the manner of how the rules are to be applied.

8. *Finally, traditional manuals adopt an essentially analytic presentation which may eventually aid the pupil in grasping the structure of ready-made sentence patterns, but which is of little value and use to him for the* construction *of such phrases.* When it is a question of oral and written expression in a second language, or even a question of written expression in the mother tongue, the pupil is constantly faced with constructing novel sentences and as a result has need for precise rules.

We ought to be clear that a number of the gaps concerning the content or the form of traditional grammars indicate that a number of coursebooks used for the teaching of a second language were originally conceived for the teaching of the mother tongue. In the latter, authors had in mind simply to lead the pupil towards analysing constructions which he already knew how to use spontaneously, and then to correct his most common errors against the norm. They saw no need to present information on oral language usage which, as far as they were concerned, the pupil already knew too well, nor to give rules for nominalization or the construction of causative sentences which pupils constantly used. This is not at all the same problem for students of a foreign language who have no intuitive knowledge or practice of the structures of the second language which is being taught to them. For such pupils one cannot do without providing all the necessary information for the construction of spoken or written utterances nor without presenting this information as explicitly as possible. G. Helbig clearly explains the difference between the necessary qualities of a mother tongue grammar and those required by a grammar of a foreign language: 'Although the first may content itself with taking note of constructions which are for the most part correct, the second has a far greater task. It has to provide a system of rules as explicit as possible for the construction of sentences. In fact, the person who learns a foreign language cannot construct such sentences without the help of such a system of rules, for in contradistinction to the person who studies his own mother tongue, the second language learner lacks any feeling for that language, any linguistic competence.'[43]

Finally traditional grammars do not provide the teacher with a satisfactory description of the language he is teaching, nor provide for the pupil a sufficient description of the language which he needs to learn. It is quite natural therefore, that teachers turn against linguists, who for almost fifty years under the influence of de Saussure, of Palmer (whose work has been far too long ignored), and Bloomfield, have been elaborating new models of grammar able to provide better descriptions both of the content and the form of languages that were to be taught. As far as methodology is concerned, traditional grammar, as with other models we shall examine, was bound to a particular conception of the acquisition of a second language. *Both courses and grammars were based on the hypothesis that one knew a language once one had mastered its forms and rules.* This is the reason why, in a grammar of French intended for foreign learners,[44] personal pronouns were taught in the following way:

(a) *Table of forms with translation*[45]

Subject	Direct Object	Indirect Object	Reflexive
je	me	me	me
ich	mich	mir	mich
io	mi, me	mi, me	mi, me
I	me	to, with etc. me	myself
tu	te	te	te
du	dich	dir	dich
tu	ti, te	ti, te	ti, te
you	you	to, with etc. you	yourself

etc.

(b) *Rules with examples*[46]

General Rule: pronoun(s) are placed in front of the verb with the exception of affirmative imperatives.

---

je lave   j'ai lavé
je le vois   je l'ai vu
je lui donne   je lui ai donné
je le lui donne   je le lui ai donné
je ne le lui donne pas je ne le lui ai pas donné

but: Écoute-moi! Donne-le-lui!

---

etc.

(c) *Exercises and Tests*[47]

45. *Replace the noun(s) in italics with appropriate pronouns.*
J'achète *ce livre*—J'ai remercié *mon oncle*—J'ai cueilli *les fleurs du jardin*—J'ai regardé attentivement *ce tableau*—J'ai donné *mon portemonnaie à Paul*—J'ai envoyé *cette lettre au directeur*, etc. (in all 19 items for exercise 45 and 22 for exercise 46).

Adopting such a mode of presentation is to admit implicitly that the meaning and usage of French personal pronouns can be properly brought out by translation. This is clearly false because, depending on the particular verb, *him* or *to him* can equally well be translated by *le* as by *lui*. It is also to admit that it is sufficient to know the forms, their combinational rules and their places of occurrence in order to know how to use them, since immediately after the presentation stage, the student passes on to a series of exercises and tests without any intermediate phase of systematic practice. In fact one cannot treat as a learning exercise a test which, without any kind of introduction, gives you a choice between twenty or so forms (*je*, *me*, *ta*, *te*, etc.) in thirty or so possible combinations (*me le*, *te le*, *le lui*, etc.) in four different positions in relation to the verb(s) (*je le prends*, *je l'ai pris*, *prends-le*, *je le fais prendre*). Is it enough to present two exercises, in total covering 41 items, to teach a system which is as complex as this? In fact these are not exercises at all, but tests of knowledge, if quite inadequate ones. What is more, nowhere is any indication given of those combinations which are peculiar to the spoken language (ʒəl for *je le*, ʒənlə for *je ne le*, etc.), and no exercises are suggested with the aim of helping the student acquire the automatic and indispensable phrases of everyday conversation. So much so that the student, if he has no chance of spending any time in a francophone country is reduced to announcing je . . . ne . . . le prendrai pas. As a result one turns out pupils who, to cite an old example, know perfectly well the five hundred pages or so of Zandvoort's *Descriptive Grammar of Contemporary English*, but as soon as they arrive in England are incapable of understanding their interlocutors and of making themselves understood to them. Pupils accumulate large quantities of information about the French language or the English language, but quite clearly have not mastered that language.

Realizing the difficulty they were in, teachers turned towards the psychologists and the psycholinguists who had just begun to elaborate new models for language learning: Skinner's Behaviourist Theory[48] and Chomsky's Cognitive Theory[49] in particular.

NOTES

1 cf. int. al. W. N. Francis: 'Revolution in Grammar' 1954 and S. R. Levin: 'Comparing traditional and structural Grammar' 1960.

2 Note: although this distinction between *presentation* and *content* is sometimes arbitrarily drawn, it is worthwhile making here for the sake of the argument.

3 J. C. Chevalier: 'Quelle grammaire enseigner?' p. 21.

4 Quoted in Grévisse: *Précis de grammaire française* p. 119.

5 Grévisse op. cit. p. 108

6 Grévisse op. cit. pp. 29–30.

7 Grévisse op. cit. p. 135.

8 cf. G. Gougenheim, R. Michea, P. Rivenc, A. Sauvageot; *L'élaboration du français fondamental (1er degré), Étude sur l'établissement d'un vocabulaire et d'une grammaire de base* p. 228.

9 P. M. Richard and W. Hall: *Anglais seconde langue, classe de 4ᵉ* p. 26.

10 P. M. Richard and W. Hall op. cit. p. 96.

11 From the preface to M. Csecsy: *De la linguistique à la pédagogie, le verbe français* p. 7.

12 M. Csecsy op. cit.

13 J. Dubois: *Grammaire structurale du français; nom et pronom* p. 21.

14 G. Mauger: *Grammaire pratique de français d'aujourd'hui, langue parlée, langue écrite.*

15 G. Mauger op. cit. p. 16.

16 L. F. and A. P. Nilsen: *A transformational approach to composition* p. iii.

17 G. Mauger op. cit. p. 38.

18 cf. N. Ruwet: '*Note sur la syntaxe du pronom en et d'autres sujets apparentés*'.

19 G. Mauger op. cit. pp. 138 and 187.

20 Grévisse op. cit. p. 217.

21 G. Mauger op. cit. pp. 259–260.

22 cf. U. Egli and E. Roulet: 'L'expression des relations d'ergativité et de transitivité dans une grammaire générative transformationelle du français.'

23 Grévisse op. cit. pp. 4–10.

24 cf. P. and M. Léon: *Introduction à la phonétique corrective.*

25 Grévisse op. cit. p. 25.

26 R. Galisson: 'L'apprentissage systématique du vocabulaire et inventaire thématique et syntagmatique du français fondamental'.

27 G. Mauger op. cit. p. 1.

28 Ibid p. 306.

29 K. Schap: 'Pronoun Stress and the Composition Teacher' p. 172.

30 Grévisse op. cit. pp. 57, 75, 83, 115, 140, 227, 242, 247, 250.

31 E. Schaap: *English Grammar and Noun Idioms for Foreigners* pp. 3, 23, 50, 74, 137, 146, 160, 165.

32 Grévisse op. cit. p. 87.

33 Ibid p. 140.

34 Ibid p. 135.

35 L. de Meuron and C. Bron: *Grammaire française.*

36 H. Mitterand: 'Observations sur les prédéterminants du nom'. J. C. Chevalier: 'Eléments pour une description du groupe nominal, les prédéterminants du substantif.'

37 Chevalier op. cit. p. 126.

38 E. Schaap op. cit. Chapter III pp. 14–22.

39 Peytard and Genouvrier: *Linguistique et enseignement du français* p. 86.

40 N. Chomsky: Introduction (pp. x–xi) to P. Roberts: *English Syntax.*

41 cf. R. B. Lees: *The Grammar of English Nominalizations* and J. Dubois: *Grammaire structurale du français, le verbe.*

42 cf. M. Grévisse: op. cit. pp. 18–20. *Grammaire Larousse du français contemporain* pp. 50–53. G. Mauger op. cit. pp. 27–28.

43 G. Helbig: 'Zur Anwendbarkeit moderner linguistischer Theorien im Fremdsprachenunterricht und zu den Beziehungen zwischen Sprach- und Lerntheorien' p. 294.

44 L. de Meuron and C. Bron op. cit.

45 L. de Meuron and C. Bron op. cit. p. 63.

46   Ibid p. 65.
47   Ibid p. 66.
48   cf. B. F. Skinner: *Verbal Behavior*.
49   cf. N. Chomsky: Review of B. F. Skinner: *Verbal Behavior* in *Language* 35.

2

Structuralist Grammar

It is not possible to review here all those recent models of grammar which have served as a basis for the development of teaching material. In avoiding both the isolated attempts of grammarians like Damourette and Pichon[1] to apply their theory or their method to a single language, and the work of linguists like Guillaume[2] which has not been systematically applied to language teaching, what we have done is only to look closely at those models of sufficient general interest because of their development, the number of languages which they have been used even partially to describe, and the extent of the teaching material which they have inspired, namely, structuralist grammar and transformational generative grammar; two models which today dominate both general linguistics and the application of linguistics to language teaching. It is possible to object that we are not treating here the contribution of the German school of Glinz and Weisgerber[3] which has exercised and continues to exercise today a great influence on language teaching in German speaking countries; H. D. Erlinger has treated this extensively in a recent work[4] and W. Abraham[5] and K. H. Bausch[6] have pointed out its drawbacks.

The useful label of structuralist grammar permits the bringing together of models of analysis containing certain differences of approach: Wells' Immediate Constituent grammar, Harris' Distributional Grammar and Pike's Tagmemic Grammar. As Postal has shown,[7] all these models can be seen to form variants of a single structuralist approach to the analysis of language and they have for the most part provided broadly similar contributions to modern language teaching.

In order to avoid the dangers implicit in traditional grammar, American structuralists had as their aim:

(a) to describe the current spoken language of an individual or of a community,

(b) to limit the area of language to be described by emphasizing language form as the single objective, observable and verifiable aspect of language, thus relegating *meaning* to a subordinate place,

(c) to carry out this programme of description by means of a systematic, objective and rigorous procedure allowing the analyst to derive the grammar of a language from a corpus of recorded data in a quasi mechanical way. The process usually followed four stages:

(1) Field recordings of a corpus of data as representative as possible of the language under study.

(2) Segmentation of the utterances of the corpus at different levels: phoneme, morpheme, 'word', group, clause, sentence.

(3) Listing of an inventory of forms thus obtained from each level and stating the distribution of the forms.

(4) Classifying the forms and utterances of the language being studied. Only such an essentially taxonomic method could enable them, it was thought, to avoid the normative, logicosemantic, and graphical aberrations of traditional grammar and to concentrate scientifically, without any preconceived categorization, on the individual structure of the language under study. It is this approach which Harris was to describe in detail in his book *Methods in Structural Linguistics*, i.e. the method to follow for distribution analysis, and which Longacre in his *Grammar Discovery Procedures* was to carry out for tagmemic analysis.

In this way, an inventory and classification is obtained of grammatical structures which occur systematically, in Delattre's phrase, in the form of a framework of slots.[8] Grammar no longer consists of a collection of rules as was the case with traditional grammar but rather as a list of structures.

It seems then as if structuralist grammar would be likely to avoid the principal drawbacks of traditional grammar and as such might furnish, both by its content and by its form, a solid basis for modern language teaching.

(A) Content

1. *In that it studies utterances recorded in the field, structuralist grammar describes a language in use in a particular community at a particular time.* Under its influence the 'Usage Movement' developed in the United States in the 1930s; the work of the movement is exemplified in works such as Leonard, *Current English Usage* (1932),

Marckwardt, *Facts about Current English Usage* (1938) and Fries, *American English Grammar, The Grammatical Structures of Present Day American English with Special References to Social Differences or Class Dialects* (1940); in themselves revealing titles. Though the movement has been slower to develop in Europe, nonetheless a large number of the published language teaching courses of the last twenty years have as their aim to teach the language of daily usage; see, for example, titles like *A Guide to Patterns and Usage in English* (1954),[9] *Realistic English* (1968)[10] or *L'allemand tel qu'on le parle* (1968).[11] The authors of the audio-visual method *Voix et Images de France* based their choice of language to be taught—grammatical constructions, lexis, pronunciation—on a systematic and statistical study of a corpus of data of the language used in France in the 1950s.[12] Parallel to this notion of 'usage', the notion of stylistic levels of language has been progressively introduced (e.g. formal written language, informal written language, formal spoken language, informal spoken language) distinctions which play very important roles in the teaching of languages.[13] One of the novel aspects of G. Mauger's: *Grammaire pratique du français d'aujourd'hui*, lies in the fact that the course presents a much more extended range of paraphrases than is usual in traditional manuals and indicates for each of these the appropriate stylistic level: *Où tu vas? Tu vas où?* (with the note: popular spoken French) *Dis-moi où est-ce que Pierre va?* (informal spoken French), etc.[14] In a similar way, in present-day taped language courses no one has any qualms about presenting the student with authentic recordings of spoken language from a number of quite different styles: cf. Dickinson and Mackin's *Varieties of Spoken English*.

2. *Structuralist grammar describes the spoken language which the pupil needs as an instrument of communication.* This contribution is particularly felt in the area of morphology where a systematic description of the features of the spoken language is usually given. Taking an example we have already used, that of the markers of the present tense and plural number in English, Martinet in his *Initiation pratique à l'anglais* (1947) begins by giving the forms and distribution of spoken language features:

—general rule: [z]
    but   [s] following [p, f, t, θ, k]
    and   [iz] following [s, z, ʃ, ʒ,][15]

So far as spoken French is concerned, thanks to the work of Dubois and Csecsy,[16] we have available for the first time a systematic description of the markers of gender, number and person which can contribute directly to the construction of structural exercises for the classroom or the language laboratory. Even before these descriptions were undertaken, applied linguists in the United States like Marty and Dostert had published courses of structural exercises in the 1950s[17] which were based on a previous study of the nature of the spoken language.

3. *Structuralist descriptions were the first to provide analyses of phonological systems which could serve as a basis for the systematic teaching of pronunciation,[18] and studies of phonemic-graphemic correspondences which could in turn furnish a much more solid basis for extending the methodology of teaching reading.[19]* We shall not, however, concentrate on this particular point which goes beyond our area of study.

(B) Form

1. *Structuralist grammar sets up precise and verifiable definitions in that it is based exclusively on formal and distributional criteria.* Taking again as an example parts of speech, every English speaker is easily able to identify the parts of speech to which the lexemes in the following sentence belong:

> *The slithy toves did gyre and gimble in the wabe*

despite the fact that they were created as neologisms by Lewis Carroll and therefore ought to have no meaning. Sentences like this are proof that it was unnecessary, in the view of structuralist linguistics, to have recourse to meaning as did traditional grammar, in order to define parts of speech. The particular words (of the example) are characterized by formal features, e.g. the final *s* on *toves*, and by distributional features, e.g. the position of *tove* between *the slithy* and *did gyre*. Paul Roberts introduced his definitions of parts of speech in a similar way in his book *Patterns of English*; 'if words occur regularly in the same patterns—the same positions in sentences, we say that they belong to the same *form class* or to the same structure words. In English there are four form classes, we call them *nouns, verbs, adjectives,* and *adverbs.* They are called *form classes* because many of them have special forms—endings and the like—which mark them off one from another'.[20]

    2. *Structuralist grammar presents linguistic units in structures or patterns.* In criticizing the analytical approach of traditional manuals, Hornby puts forward the advantages of his new method of presentation: 'analysis is helpful, but the learner is, or should be, more concerned with sentence-building. For this he needs to know the patterns of English sentences and to be told which words enter into which patterns'.[21] What is put forward then is a framework of sentence-slots as in the following sentence:

Suzanne	bought	a new dress	on Saturday

which the pupil can modify by substituting new elements in one or other of the slots (substitution exercises)

my mother	bought	this new dress	on Saturday
my mother	bought	this hat	on Saturday
my mother	bought	this hat	yesterday
— — — —	— — —	— — — — —	— — — — —

    etc

or by changing the order of the slots without changing either the number or the nature of the constituents,

On Saturday	Suzanne	bought	this new dress

or by transforming certain constituents and by changing the order of the slots without modifying the number of the items,

Suzanne	bought	it	on Saturday

or finally by modifying the number of slots,

Suzanne	did	not	buy	the new dress	on Saturday

thus producing different types of transformational exercise.[22] This technique in particular rapidly produces a quantity of substitution tables which allow a large number of sentences to be derived from a single pattern presented in the form of a series of slots and a limited number of elements.[23] These substitution tables have, incidentally, in a curious way found their theoretical justification in Pike's Tagmemic Grammar; Valdman makes the point that: 'Tagmemics gives us the theory we need to design structural drills of the type often called substitution drills'.[24]

It appeared that such great progress was being made both in the analysis of form and of content of the grammar that the structuralists were not at all reluctant to maintain that they had finally discovered a precise and complete model which could definitively replace traditional grammar, both in terms of language description and of language teaching.[25] This success appeared all the more assured given that structural linguistics, ever since Bloomfield's *Language*, has reflected a behaviourist concept of language learning. Principally under the influence of the psychologist Skinner, this concept underpinned a model of learning concerned with enabling pupils to acquire the necessary automatisms for the practice of spoken language in daily communication.[26]

Both audio-visual methods and courses of structural exercises which have increased greatly in number since the 1940s derive from this coming-together of linguistic and psychological research. Structuralist grammar provided the framework of slots within sentence patterns which could be manipulated by substitution and transformation operations. Behaviourist psychology, with its theory of conditioning, proposed a mechanical process of habit-formation through which the phases of stimulus-response-reinforcement would determine the formulation of structure drills and would lead the student to the acquisition of these structures. In this way the deductive mode of presentation of traditional manuals:

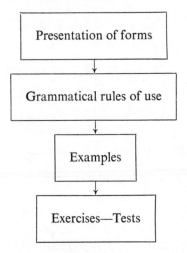

was replaced by an inductive method

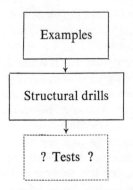

Examining the contribution of structuralist grammar to language teaching today with the advantage of a certain amount of hindsight and taking account of Chomsky's work, progress beyond traditional grammar appears less extensive than one might have thought in the 1950s. Indeed, it even appears that in certain areas structuralist grammar represents a step backwards in comparison with traditional grammar. Chomsky makes this clear in his preface to Paul Roberts' work *English Syntax* (p. xi). Modern structural linguistics has reached levels of vigour that often exceed those of traditional grammar, and it has revealed previously unrecognized aspects of linguistic structure. However, it provides little insight into the processes of formation and interpretation of sentences. Study of these questions has been outside the scope of modern structuralism, which has limited itself, almost completely, to the system of inventories of elements (phonemes, morphemes) and to analytic procedures that may assist in determining these elements. There has been some discussion of syntactic patterns, but it has been fairly primitive as compared with traditional grammar.

In other words, if structuralist grammars presented more precise, explicit descriptions than traditional grammars, thanks to their strict adherence to formal and distributional criteria, this gain was paid for by very heavy sacrifices, in that structuralist grammars avoided fundamental problems which were only taken up by trans-formational generative grammars. If structuralist grammars constituted a step forward from traditional grammar as far as language *form* was concerned, in the area of language *content* they marked rather a step backward.

We now need to examine in detail the most striking gaps in structuralist grammars; in particular their treatment of language content.

1. *Structuralist grammars present an incomplete description of the grammatical system of language. In simply providing an inventory of forms and constructions which appear in a necessarily limited corpus, they do not provide the rules needed to construct an infinite range of grammatical sentences.* No one argues that the lists of basic structures provided by any distributional or tagmemic grammar do not constitute good working tools for the beginning of the language learning process through audio-visual or audio-lingual methods. If, however, one admits that to know a language, i.e. to be able to understand and produce an infinity of utterances, these beginning steps need to be followed by a stage nowadays of ever greater importance, where creative usage of language has to be developed in the pupil,[27] then as Chomsky has clearly shown,[28] structuralist grammar in its inability to account satisfactorily for this creativity is bound to fail.

2. *Structuralist grammars attach excessive weight to grammatical facts of secondary importance (e.g. morphological or morphophono-logical rules) just as traditional grammar attached too much importance to secondary graphic facts, and thus neglect important generalizations.* A striking fact is that in the first structuralist description of French written in 1948, 56 pages long, about ten are given over to phonology, thirty or so to morphophonology and morphology and only ten to syntax.[29] Whatever the linguistic value and pedagogical importance

may be of the discovery of the marks of gender and number in spoken French, we are nonetheless dealing with an element of secondary importance in the language system, much less crucial for the teaching process than the rules for construction of utterances in the area of the verb phrase. Both the structural descriptions of the French verb[30] we have already mentioned, although they have the advantage of dealing with the spoken language code, nonetheless like traditional grammars provide large quantities of information on the morphology of the verb but all too little on its syntax.

3. *In structuralist grammars much more so than in traditional grammars, syntactic relations very often receive slight treatment.* In descriptions such as Hall's for French, or Hill's for English,[31] what one finds set out in a neat inventory are the principal constructions of the language; nowhere, however, are any indications found of those relationships holding between the constructions which are quite obvious to native-speakers. As an example one finds

> (a) the active declarative affirmative construction:
> The government refused permission for the demonstration
> (b) the active declarative negative construction:
> The government did not refuse permission for the demonstration
> (c) the active interrogative affirmative construction:
> Did the government refuse permission for the demonstration?
> (d) the passive declarative affirmative construction:
> This demonstration was refused permission by the government, etc.

Each of these constructions is presented *in isolation* without indicating those extremely useful and productive rules for language teaching which allow speakers to shift from one construction to the other.

Similarly, different constructions such as:

> (a) I expected it
> (b) someone fired the man
> (c) the man quit work,

are presented, without, however, providing rules for the formulation of a complex construction from the three component propositions, i.e.

> (d) I expected the man who quit work to be fired.[32]

What has to be made clear, then, is that structuralist grammars did not provide sufficient information for the pupil to learn how to formulate new constructions, in particular, complexes, nor did they provide the basis for the systematic teaching of writing, any more that traditional grammars had done.

4. *In so far as structuralist grammars only describe the surface structure of sentences, they clearly cannot adequately take account of important grammatical facts.* Chomsky's well-known example makes this point:[33] if one defines a grammatical structure as a series of constituents, the two sentences

| John | is | easy | to | please |
| John | is | eager | to | please |

present the same structure. This runs contrary to native-speaker intuition for whom in the first sentence *John* is the object of *please*, (one can say: it is easy to please John), while in the second *John* is the subject. Ruwet provides a further example in French:[34]

> Pierre a conseillé à Jean de consulter un spécialiste
> Pierre a promis à Jean de consulter un spécialiste

In the same way both show an identical surface structure; in the first sentence, however, the two verbs have different subjects (it is Peter who advises and John who consults), while in the second sentence the two verbs have the same subject (Peter both promises and consults). If one now takes the noun phrase *The fear of the enemy* in the sentence

> The fear of the enemy overthrew our plans

we see a case of syntactic ambiguity which structuralist grammar cannot handle and which becomes clear from the two utterances:

> The enemy was afraid: this overthrew our plans
> We were afraid of the enemy: this overthrew our plans.

What is necessary, therefore, is to make pupils aware of such grammatical facts because the comprehension of the utterance and often its correct translation into another language (for example, in German *die Angst der Feinde* and *die Angst vor den Feinden*) depends on the distinction. Traditional grammar, not relying on a surface structure analysis of such sentences, was well able to distinguish the two constructions; subjective genitive in the first case, objective genitive in the second, and would have gone on to analyse correctly the other examples which have been cited. One is now in a better position to understand Chomsky's affirmation that structuralist grammar represented in certain respects a step backward in the area of the analysis of content and meaning.

It is worth examining more closely the consequences for language teaching of this omission in structural grammars. R. H. Wagner makes the following point: 'Hence if "patterns" are established solely on the basis of surface structure, it is to be expected that a particular pattern will collapse several deep structures with different interpretations and different transformational potentials.'[35] In analysing a structure taught by Hornby in his *A Guide to Patterns and Usage in English*, and presenting it as follows:

	wanted		(a)
	wished		(b)
Bill	helped	John to paint the picture	(c)
	taught		(d)
	reminded		(e)

Wagner has shown conclusively that such a substitution table mixes together sentences of quite different deep structures, which admit of different transformations in English and have different translation equivalents in other languages.[36] Sentences (a) and (b) only permit the cleft sentence transformation which produces structures of the order:

(f) What Bill wanted was for John to paint the picture.

For sentence (e) it is necessary to add a preposition:

(g) What Bill reminded John of was to paint a picture.

The application of other transformations to sentences (a) to (e) will reveal further differences. As for the translation of the sentences into German, they present at least three different types of structure:

(a^1) (b^1) Bill wollte (wünschte) dass John das Bild malt
(c^1) (d^1) Bill half (lehrte) John, das Bild zu malen
(e^1) Bill erinnerte John daran, das Bild zu malen[37]

In putting together within the same structural exercise sentences which have such great underlying differences despite their identical surface structure, the author runs the grave risk of leading the pupils to make false generalizations in the interpretation, use, transformation and translation of such sentences. R. Jacobson comes to an analogous conclusion after having examined sentence structures of the type

$$NP + Vtr + NP + \left(\left\{ \begin{array}{c} OF \\ TO \\ FOR \end{array} \right\} \right) + NP$$

and their treatment in Lado and Fries' book *English Sentence Patterns:* 'the learner therefore fails to make valid generalizations and in order to master the lesson he depends entirely on the recognition, the repetition, and the production of each individual occurrence with the false expectation that all of this helps him acquire automatic control of the entire problem. At best the student produces the examples given in the book but without actually accomplishing the mastery of the patterns involved. Such mastery can only be achieved if the learner internalizes the rules which determine the proper choice'.[38]

5.   *Where structuralist grammars generally provide insufficient explanation to guarantee clear comprehension and correct usage, the learner is much more easily led into error.* As Wagner's example above indicates, the presentation of a new structure by means of examples and structural exercises or substitution tables often leaves inexplicit precisely that information which is indispensable for the usage, transformation and translation of the structures in question. In this way such grammars fail to provide the pupil with the means of correctly expressing himself. Lamendella makes the point in his review of *Modern English*: 'Explanations of grammatical structures in ESL texts are generally insufficient to permit the student to understand what is involved in correct use of a structure'.[39] Only explicit rules of sentence construction can fill that particular gap.

6. *Structuralist grammar does not provide the teacher with criteria to determine grammaticality and degrees of grammaticality of utterances.* It is not a question here of regretting the absence of the absolute norms behind which traditional teachers and grammarians took refuge. We can agree with the structuralists that there are as many norms as there are levels of language and dialects. What one has to do for each structure is to determine whether it is grammatical at a particular level and if it is not, to determine what its degree of grammaticality or deviation is in relation to other grammatical utterances of the language system at that level. Two areas of information are indispensable in at least two respects for a language teaching course: the choice of structures to teach and the control of the pupils' knowledge at different stages in the learning process. What is not possible,

then, is to stick to a system of binary assessment between what is accurate and what is incorrect. As Corder points out; 'it is clear that from a practical point of view it is not sufficient to know that an error has been made. In itself such a statement has no value. We can only derive information from students' errors if we are capable of describing them in an adequate manner. Description needs to precede correction'.[40] One has to be able to be precise about the type and the degree of the error in indicating the type and number of the rules which have been omitted or violated. No structuralist grammar is able to provide this information.

We can refer again here to an already cited example for the purpose of illustrating this point; viz. interrogative forms with *où, quand, comment, combien* in spoken French. Simply to know how one will meet the following forms in contemporary French and their frequency of occurrence is not enough:

où va ton père?	il va où?
où va-t-il?	où il va?
où ton père va-t-il?	où c'est qu'il va?
où est-ce qu'il va?	où qu'il va?[41]

What has to be done first is to determine what structures to teach in a course aimed at particular level(s) of language; this presupposes a grammatical description of the language system at each level.[42] Once the level of learners' knowledge is controlled in this way, and given that these learners will produce forms different from those which have been taught, one can then go on to determine precisely the degree of grammaticality of each sentence. Thus if one considers *où va-t-il?* as the only fully grammatical sentence at the particular level concerned in the chosen language, then the form *où va-il* results from the omission of a morphophonological rule, the form *où il va* results from the omission of the pronominal inversion rule, *il va où* stems from the same omission aggravated by the absence of the rule of preposition of the interrogative morpheme, etc. Only a system of explicit rules can provide important information of this kind for the teacher.

7. *In ignoring notions of degree of grammaticality and deviance, structuralist grammar does not provide an adequate descriptive instrument for the two areas playing a more and more important role in research into applied linguistics and language teaching: error analysis and stylistic analysis.* The previous section[43] relates to the first area, but for the second, Herndon poses the problem in these terms: 'All

forms of creative and imaginative writing allow the writer certain liberties with English grammatical patterns (. . .). When rules are broken by poets and authors of recognized worth it is safe to say that such rule breaking is done with determination and care and is not simply playful disregard of authority or, worse, carelessness. The best way to demonstrate this to students is to consider carefully which rules have been broken and then to understand what effect the deviation produces'.[44] We shall return to this point in the next chapter.

8. *Structuralist grammar does not provide satisfactory bases for two other important areas of applied linguistics in language teaching, contrastive analysis and translation, since in asserting the individual character of each language and in remaining at the surface structure level of utterances it is prevented from establishing a middle level between the systems of two or more languages.* As Di Pietro points out,[45] 'Even from the start the limitations of structural linguistics were evident with regard to CA. The insistence on defining phonological and grammatical categories solely in terms of individual languages made detailed contrastive statements laborious, if not theoretically impossible, to phrase. Only through difficult modification of the theory could the phonemes of one language ever be equated with the phonemes of another, or the morphemes of one be compared to the morphemes of another. In discrediting an earlier non-rigorous view of universal grammar by insisting on the definition of a language's forms in terms of its own structure, structural linguists found themselves in difficulty when it came to formulating the common ground of language similarity which is a vital foundation for CA'. In fact, if one accepts with Lado[46] the hypothesis by which one can predict those structures which will cause problems during language learning by comparing the system of the second language with that of the mother tongue of the pupils, one is entitled to doubt seriously whether it would be sufficient for this merely to present in parallel two sets of surface structures from the two languages in question. This was what was done in the first works in the *Contrastive Structure Series*[47] and Politzer does the same in the following table:[48]

I permit him to study	Je lui permets d'étudier
I forbid him to study	Je lui defends d'étudier
I want him to study	Je veux qu'il étudie

Nickel and Wagner explain very clearly why this type of contrastive analysis is insufficient for language teaching: 'the results of such comparisons are certainly highly relevant for language tuition but they tend to over-emphasize differences in the surface structures of the languages compared while neglecting more fundamental differences in the underlying deep structures. The following consideration, however, appears to us to be of even greater significance. If one regards speech as a series of processes directed by the rule system of the language (i.e. by its grammar), it follows that interferences occur primarily between the various processes which generate the structure of individual sentences. These processes are in turn dependent on the choices in the rule systems. The conclusion to be drawn from this consideration is that *the primary task of contrastive analysis must be the comparison of rules and rule systems and not of the structures determined by them*'.[49] In wishing to go beyond the stage of superficial comparisons to predict in some valid way the errors that pupils are likely to make, it is necessary to propose a point of contrast between two or more languages, for example, the idea of deep structure, and then to compare the two systems of explicit rules formulated within the framework of the same theory.

10. *Although semantics goes outside the framework of this study, the point should be made that the exclusion of the treatment of meaning by American structuralist linguistics on the grounds that it could not be handled objectively by scientific methods, effectively prevents the provision of necessary information for the systematic teaching of lexis and more generally of oral and written comprehension.* Galisson makes the point that: 'vocabulary is the poor cousin in modern language teaching and has undergone much less of a revolution in teaching than has either grammar or phonetics in the light of modern linguistic research'.[50]

From the views put forward here, it is clear that nowadays there has been a considerable movement away from the enthusiasm which both general and applied linguists showed for structuralist grammar at the beginning of the 1950s. This sudden shift has, however, surprised teachers and placed them in a very uncomfortable situation. Both in the United States and then in Europe they had converted themselves only with considerable difficulty (after a good deal of reticence and a good deal of effort) to structural linguistics, which had been presented to them as a panacea, only now to discover in it considerable numbers of errors. The same is true for methodology where it will be sufficient to point out three major omissions.

(1) *The accent placed by early structuralists on formal and distributional criteria at the expense of situational and semantic factors, in addition to the importance accorded by Skinnerian psychologists to a theory of step-by-step learning, led both teachers and pupils to manipulate structures as an end in themselves while neglecting the area of their application in everyday life.* Newmark makes the comment that: 'inspection of language textbooks designed by linguists reveals an increasing emphasis in recent years on structural drills in which pieces of language are isolated from the linguistic and social contexts which make them meaningful and useful to the learner. The more we know about language the more such drills we have been tempted to make. If one compares, say, the spoken language textbooks devised by linguists during the Second World War with some of the recent textbooks devised by linguists, one is at once struck by the shift of emphasis from connected situational dialogue to disconnected structural exercise'.[51] There was thus a great increase in the 1950s and 1960s of boring mechanical drills producing pupils who were often incapable of using these structures correctly in the variety of situations of daily communication.

(2) *Structuralists led teachers to think that language was the only variable in language pedagogy and thus to neglect the problems of language learning and teaching.* F. C. Johnson makes the comment that,[52] 'if anything, linguists have been too successful for they have seduced us into the belief that language is not only the prime variable in language teaching but virtually the only variable (. . .). What it in effect meant for language teaching was that our attention was directed almost exclusively to language at the expense of, and to the neglect of, "teaching" and "learning" '. As a result: 'language teaching methodology today is virtually in the state it was 50 years ago when Harold Palmer and others were developing the concept of pattern practice'.[53] Structural linguists were not qualified to put forward a methodology of language teaching, particularly when one realizes that they were interested uniquely in the description of the language code and not in its usage. To the two traditional questions of language teaching: 'What to teach?' and 'How to teach?', they were able to reply to the first but not at all to the second. As Contreras makes clear: 'Strangely enough however, the main impact of structural linguistics on language teaching has been related to the second question, in the form of the so-called linguistic method'.[54] This method, applied in particular to audio-visual courses and language laboratory exercises, seems today, as a result of its frequently mechanical and oppressive character, to

be at odds with teachers' attempts to liberate the creative power of their pupils. 'It is evidently a problem,' Debyser notes, 'that even those methods called "new" or "modern" for the teaching of modern languages risk being considered as ultra-traditional from the point of view of general pedagogy'.[55] Linguists realized their error a little late, as W. Moulton, one of the first protagonists of the linguistic method, points out: 'To judge by what my fellow linguists and I have some-times said in the past, it might seem as though we thought that we—and we alone—knew all the answers to all the problems of language teaching. We most emphatically do not. In matters of language peda-gogy—planning lessons, designing drills, using the laboratory—we know no more than the next man and a good deal less than many. The one thing which we have to offer is linguistic theory—a rather exciting body of theory on what language is and how it works. This means that when the language teacher wants to know *what* aspects of language should be drilled, we may have some ideas worth listening to, but when he then asks *how* these things should be drilled, our ideas are worth no more than anyone else's'.[56]

(3) *Finally, one is aware today that this new methodology is based on an inadequate model of language learning, i.e. the verbal conditioning theory associated with Skinner.* Chomsky has made this point very clear in his review of Skinner's *Verbal Behavior*, i.e. that Skinnerian theory does not account in a satisfactory manner for the acquisition and creative use of language. Chomsky recalled these comments in 1964 at a conference of language teaching specialists. 'Within psy-chology, there are now many who would question the view that the basic principles of learning are well understood. Long accepted principles of association and reinforcement gestalt principles, the theory of concept formation as it has emerged in modern investiga-tion, all of these have been sharply challenged in theoretical as well as experimental work. To me it seems that the principles are not merely inadequate but probably misconceived—that they deal with marginal aspects of acquisition of knowledge and leave the central core of the problem untouched. In particular, it seems impossible to accept the concept according to which linguistic performance is a matter of habit and is acquired slowly by process of reinforcement, association and generalization.'[57]

In conclusion, critics, both in the area of linguistics and method-ology, have been severe. As a result, one begins to understand how it is that the most recent manuals and courses of language teaching refer less and less to structuralist grammar.

NOTES

1 J. Damourette and E. Pichon: *Des mots à la pensée—Essai de grammaire de la langue française.*

2 G. Guillaume: 'Le problème de l'article et sa solution dans la langue française; Temps et verbe'.

3 H. Glinz: *Die innere Form des Deutschen.* L. Weisgerber: *Grundzüge der inhaltsbezogenen Grammatik.*

4 H. D. Erlinger: *Sprachwissenschaft und Schulgrammatik.*

5 W. Abraham: Neue Wege der Angewandten Sprachwissenschaft—Erkennungs- und Erzeugungsgrammatik.

6 K. H. Bausch: Report to a Symposium of the Council of Europe on 'La place de la grammaire dans les méthodes modernes d'enseignement des langues vivantes' Brussels (16–20.11.1970). K. H. Bausch: *The Teaching of German in German Schools and Current Trends in Linguistics in German Universities.*

7 P. Postal: *Constituent Structure, a Study of Contemporary Models of Syntactic Description.*

8 P. Delattre: 'La notion de structure et son utilité' p. 7.

9 A. S. Hornby: *A Guide to Patterns and Usage in English.*

10 B. Abbs, V. Cook and M. Underwood: *Realistic English.*

11 J. Gerighausen and H. Martin: *L'allemand tel qu'on le parle.*

12 G. Gougenheim, R. Michea, P. Rivenc and A. Sauvageot: *L'élaboration du français fondamental (1er degré): Etude sur l'établissement d'un vocabulaire et d'une grammaire de base.*

13 cf. Chapter IV of H. B. Allen (ed.) *Readings in Applied English Linguistics.*

14 G. Mauger op. cit. p. 380.

15 A. Martinet: *Initiation pratique à l'anglais* pp. 27, 36, 37.

16 J. Dubois: op. cit. M. Csecsy: op. cit.

17 F. Marty: *Spoken and Written French for the Language Laboratory* 1958. L. Dostert: *Spoken French, Basic Course* 1956.

18 P. Delattre: *Principes de phonétique française à l'usage des étudiants anglo-américains.* P. Léon: *Laboratoire de langues et correction phonétique.* M. Léon: *Exercices systématiques de prononciation française.*

19 L. Bloomfield and C. L. Barnhart: *Let's Read.* P. Léon: *Aide-mémoire d'orthoépie.*

20 P. Roberts: *Patterns of English* p. 12.

21 A. S. Hornby: *A Guide to Patterns and Usage in English* p. v.

22 cf. F. Requedat: *Les exercices structuraux.*

23 cf. F. G. French: *English in Tables* or H. V. George: 101 *Substitution Tables for Students of English.*

24 A. Valdman: 'Structural Drill and the Language Laboratory' p. 12. S. Belasco: 'Les structures grammaticales orales' p. 37.

25   cf. W. N. Francis: 'Revolution in Grammar'.

26   cf. Wilga Rivers: *The Psychologist and the Foreign Language Teacher*.

27   cf. R. Hester (ed.) *Teaching a Living Language*.

28   esp. in *Language and Mind*.

29   Robert A. Hall: *French*.

30   J. Dubois (op. cit.) M. Csecsy (op. cit.).

31   A. A. Hill: *Introduction to Linguistic Structures. From Sound to Sentence in English*.

32   N. Chomsky: *Topics in the Theory of Generative Grammar* pp. 52–54.

33   *Current Issues in Linguistic Theory* p. 34.

34   N. Ruwet: *Introduction à la grammaire générative* p. 325.

35   R. H. Wagner: 'The relevance of the notion of "Deep Structure" to Contrastive Analysis' p. 3.

36   R. H. Wagner (op. cit.) and *Probleme der kontrastiven Sprachwissenschaft* pp. 320–322.

37   R. H. Wagner op. cit.

38   R. Jacobson: 'The role of deep structures in language teaching' p. 157.

39   J. T. Lamendella: *Review* of W. E. Rutherford: *Modern English* p. 152.

40   S. P. Corder: 'Le rôle de l'analyse systématique des erreurs en linguistique appliquée pp. 6–7.

41   G. Gougenheim, R. Michea, P. Rivenc, A. Sauvageot op. cit. p. 228.

42   cf. A. Valdman: 'Norme pédagogique: les structures intérrogatives du français'.

43   cf. also P. Corder: 'The significance of learners' errors'.

44   J. H. Herndon: *A Survey of Modern Grammars* p. 184.

45   R. J. Di Pietro: 'Contrastive Analysis and the notions of Deep and Surface Structure' p. 66.

46   R. Lado: *Linguistics across Cultures* p. vii.

47   H. L. Kufner: *The Grammatical Structures of English and German*. F. B. Agard and R. J. Di Pietro: *The Grammatical Structures of English and Italian*.

48   R. L. Politzer: *Applied Linguistics: French* p. 107.

49   G. Nickel and R. H. Wagner: *Contrastive Linguistics and Language Teaching* p. 240.

50   Reported by J. F. Maire in 'Vers un apprentissage systématisé du Vocabulaire' p. 57.

51   L. Newmark: 'How not to interfere with language learning' p. 223.

52   F. C. Johnson: 'The failure of the discipline of linguistics in language teaching' pp. 235–236.

53   Ibid p. 236.

54   H. Contreras: 'Transformational Grammar and Language Teaching' p. 6.

55   F. Debyser: 'L'enseignement du français langue étrangère au niveau 2' p. 13.

56   W. Moulton: 'Structural Drill and the Language Laboratory', p. 5.

57   N. Chomsky: 'Linguistic Theory' p. 43.

3

Transformational Generative Grammar

Developed by Chomsky and his followers from 1955 onwards,[1] the transformational generative model appears as a synthesis of the most interesting contributions of traditional and structuralist grammar. At a time when Nelson Francis was concerned with recalling all of the faults of traditional grammars and presenting structural grammar as a revolution[2] and in so doing reflecting the opinion of the majority of linguists, Chomsky was maintaining the paradox that traditional grammar, through the aims it set itself and the information it provided, reflected a more satisfying conception of the nature of language. In 1966 in his book *Cartesian Linguistics*, he could write of transformational generative grammar that 'in many respects it seems to me quite accurate to regard the theory of transformational generative grammar as it is developing in current work as essentially a modern and more explicit version of the Port-Royal theory'.[3] But if he recognized the value of the treatment of *content* in traditional grammars, which had been misunderstood by structuralists, he nevertheless severely criticized its *form*. The vague, ambiguous or incomprehensible character of its definitions, rules and explanations indicated for Chomsky that traditional grammar had been formulated in an insufficiently precise metalanguage; everyday language enriched by a number of technical terms like *gerundive* or *subjunctive*. Only recourse to a rigorous and explicit metalanguage such as the formal propositions of logic and mathematics would enable the grammarian to formulate precise rules.[4]

As far as scientific analysis is concerned, substantial progress has been made, but one can still point out that up to now a number of serious problems concerning applications of the theory have emerged. As long as grammatical constructions were explained in everyday language as was the case with traditional grammars, or presented in the form of a series of frames and slots as with structural grammars, it was easy to teach them to pupils in the form they were. This was no longer the case when linguists began to use a metalanguage as abstract and complex as was to be found in transformational generative grammars. We will return to this problem below.

As far as structuralist grammar was concerned, Chomsky retained immediate constituent analysis as a first stage of his grammar, but went much further in satisfying the demands of precision in the formalization of his grammar. His major criticisms against structural grammar were the following:

(a) That it limited itself to the inventory and analysis of utterances from a corpus without seeking to characterize the rules which permit all native speakers to produce an infinity of grammatical utterances; i.e. their linguistic competence.

(b) That it did not take account of intuitively recognized linguistic facts, e.g. declarative, interrogative, negative and passive paraphrase relationships of a single utterance.

(c) That in remaining at the surface structure level it missed making a number of deep generalizations.[5]

In filling these gaps Chomsky conceived of transformational generative grammar as a system of rewrite rules which, beginning from the initial symbol S plus a lexicon, permitted the generation of a series of deep structure symbols containing in principle all of the necessary semantic information for the interpretation of sentences. A second group of rules called transformational rules modified the order of the symbols in these strings and assigned to each sentence a surface structure.[6]

Quite clearly, for Chomsky, there does not exist a systematic method for discovering the rules and deep structures of the transformational generative grammar of any given language. In particular he makes clear that it is impossible to attain these deep structures via direct observation and by analysis of the products of a corpus as was maintained by structuralist grammarians. For the same reason you cannot hope to extract an atom from a piece of wood by cutting it into ever smaller pieces.[7] Thus linguists could no longer content themselves with making inventories and classifications of the products of a corpus. What was necessary was for them to characterize in the form of an abstract hypothesis that system of rules which permits us to understand and generate an infinity of novel sentences. By applying the rules they could then verify that the system thus devised would allow the effective generation of all of the grammatical sentences of the language, or rather (as a check on the system), that it would not generate any ungrammatical utterances.

For scientific analysis, this constituted a step forward, but it raised serious problems as soon as one was concerned with applications of the theory. As long as one was happy with labelling directly observable facts, as was the case with traditional and structural grammars, it was easy to pass on this information, just as it was, in a language teaching course. Now when linguists utilize as the base elements of their rules and their deep structures, symbols which correspond to abstract facts and are not amenable to direct observation, this can no longer be the case.

This no doubt explains why the problem of applications of models of grammatical analysis to teaching has appeared particularly acute with the development of transformational generative linguistics.

In order to be under no illusions, it must be made quite clear that, despite its progress, Chomsky's grammar is still a considerable distance away from producing a complete solution to our problem. In fact, both at the level of theory and description and at the level of application to language teaching it raises almost as many problems as it solves. Chomsky was the first to make this point in his 1964 remarks: 'I should like to make it clear from the outset that I am participating in this conference not as an expert on any aspect of the teaching of languages, but rather as someone whose primary concern is with the structure of language and, more generally, the nature of cognitive processes. Furthermore I am frankly rather sceptical about the significance for the teaching of languages of such insights and understanding as have been obtained in linguistics and psychology. Surely the teacher of language would do well to keep informed of progress and discussion in these fields and the efforts of linguists and psychologists to approach the problems of language teaching from a principled point of view are extremely worthwhile from an intellectual as well as a social point of view. Still it is difficult to believe that either linguistics or psychology has achieved a level of theoretical understanding that might enable it to support a "technology" of language teaching'.[8] Although Chomsky has not condemned the numerous tentative attempts at applying transformational generative grammar to language teaching (he even wrote a preface for Paul Roberts' manual *English Syntax*, where, and this is significant, he does not tackle the problem of applications) one can still consider that he views such applications as premature. One ought not to forget in the account that follows that those textbooks which multiplied from

1960 onwards only reflect in an extremely partial manner the concepts and research of Chomsky and his followers.

Setting aside for the moment what transformational generative grammar has contributed, or appears to have contributed, to language teaching in the course of the last ten years, let us examine the premises and content of the courses published during this period.

1. *In that transformational generative grammar presents an overall conception of the system of language which is more accurate and more complete than other models of grammar, it ought as a result to provide better linguistic foundations for language teaching pedagogy.* This is the thesis developed among others by Owen Thomas in his book *Transformational Grammar and the Teacher of English* and by W. O'Neil in *Kernels and Transformations*; both books, however, being concerned with mother tongue teaching. For the above authors, whatever the direct application of generative transformational grammar might be to the elaboration of courses and exercises, the model leads teacher and pupil towards:

(a) a better understanding of the way the language system in general functions, and of the system of the language under study in particular.

(b) a better understanding of the way in which the human mind functions; an important gain if one expects from school education something wider than the learning of simple techniques.

Paul Roberts expresses the same idea in the notes to his programmed course of transformational generative grammar: 'It is hoped that the student who works carefully through this text will derive from it the following values:— (1) He should get an understanding of the nature of the English language and to some extent of language in general, an understanding that is valuable for its own sake (. . .). He may get some insight into the problem of how it is possible for us to learn our language and thus to function as human beings'.[9] Given the particular importance of this argument for mother tongue teaching, suggesting as it does a more educational than merely technical aspect to learning, it is doubtless equally valid for the teaching of a foreign language.

2. *It would be wrong to see transformational generative grammar as constituting for language teaching a damaging break away from grammatical models which up to now have dominated language teaching pedagogy. What it strives to do is to provide a synthesis of the most important contributions of both traditional grammar and structuralist*

grammar. This is an argument advanced by Paul Roberts in the preface of his book *English Sentences:* 'Chomsky's transformational or generative grammar is certainly one of the major developments in linguistics in recent years. It is a development particularly interesting for students and teachers of English since it goes a long way towards reconciling highly divergent views about English teaching—the linguistic and the traditional'.[10] Without stopping at this point to go further into the issue of the reconciliation between methodologies, it is clear that the reconciliations are most numerous in the area of syntax. If we consider again an earlier example, viz the treatment of the syntactic ambiguity contained within the sentence '*the hatred of the enemies*', we see that between a traditional grammar which sought to account, but in an insufficiently explicit way, for the intuitively correct distinction, subjective genitive and objective genitive, and structuralist grammar which, in seeking formal and distributional criteria, rejected such a distinction because of its logicosemantic character, Chomsky nonetheless retains the clearly important traditional distinction and makes it explicit, and thus combines together the significance of content and the precision of form.

3. *Transformational generative grammar does not simply provide a list of forms and structures as did structuralist grammar. What it does is to provide rules which, contrary to those of traditional grammar, are clear and formally explicit.* In doing so much more precise and complete information than would be found in other types of grammar is given on the construction of grammatical sentences. This is no doubt why certain textbooks for the teaching of English as a mother tongue like Paul Roberts' *English Syntax*, or for the teaching of English as a second language like W. E. Rutherford's *Modern English*, have taken up the linguists' rules. The experiments conducted by Ney and Isacenko have pointed out the advantages which one can draw from the formal rules of a transformational generative grammar for the teaching of a foreign language. Ney reports that the teaching of English grammar to Japanese students by means of a pedagogic grammar [Paul Roberts' *English Sentences*] and two linguistic descriptions [Chomsky's *Syntactic Structures* and Lees' *The Grammar of English Nominalizations*] 'resulted in an improvement in the students' ability to produce acceptable English sentences'.[11] Isacenko makes the point to those who have doubts about the abstract character of generative rules that: 'the use of an auxiliary vocabulary, the use of syntactic symbols prove to be of little difficulty. Students well understand abstract rules and see them very much as rules of a game'.

He concludes that 'in applying syntactic rules, the student begins to understand the mechanism of the language'.[12] It is nonetheless necessary to make clear that the textbooks of Roberts and Rutherford are not intended for young pupils and that Ney and Isacenko's experiments were carried out at university level.

4. *Contrary to those of traditional grammar, transformational generative rules are ordered.* As such the grammar provides a more economic and systematic description of a language. Indeed, and this is an important advantage for teaching, it is the only model which 'proposes a systematic grammatical progression',[13] as we noted a little over-hastily in 1967. Paul Roberts in his *English Syntax* presents very clearly the generative and transformational rules in the order in which they are given by Chomsky. We shall return later to the question of whether such a procedure is legitimate.

5. *Transformational generative grammar provides indispensable information for structural exercises of the transformational type which occupy an important place in language teaching pedagogy.* Moulton makes the point 'it can serve as a wonderful new source of structural drills for use in the language laboratory'[14] and Earl Rand, author of a course of structural exercises writes: 'Many of the drills are based on the transformational analysis of English found in R. B. Lees' *The Grammar of English Nominalizations*'.[15] At least in its earlier version, transformational generative grammar provides rules for optional transformations permitting the systematic derivation from kernel sentences of a range of structures, interrogative, negative, negative interrogative, passive, etc. In this there is a connection to a pedagogical technique much earlier than Chomsky, which consists of constructing a passive sentence from a corresponding active sentence. From this it is easy to understand the rapid development of a type of application different from that mentioned above under (3) where instead of providing pupils with abstract symbols and complex rules governing transformations, it is sufficient to illustrate these rules by examples, such as converting positive sentences into negative ones, actives into passives.

> L'hôtesse sert les invités L'hôtesse ne sert pas les invités
> L'hôtesse sert les invités Les invités sont servis par l'hôtesse[16]

According to the authors of this particular textbook, what this shows is that 'through a non-technical application of the principles of generative transformational grammar (this book) leads the student from the manipulation of simple sentence patterns to the production of longer and more complex structures'.[17] No doubt an efficient pedagogic technique, but it is difficult to see how one can talk of applying transformational generative grammar if in order to justify perfectly defensible pedagogic motives, one abandons the formal apparatus which in fact characterizes this transformational generative model.

6. *Transformational generative grammar provides rules which allow for the systematic construction of complex sentences; as such it provides an excellent basis for the teaching of writing.* It is true that the first version of transformational generative grammar did present transformational rules (called generalized transformational rules) which permitted the systematic combination of several propositions into a complex sentence. In an article appropriately entitled *How Little Sentences Grow into Big Ones*, K. W. Hunt writes 'A transformational generative grammar also gives you explicit directions on how to make big sentences out of little ones',[18] he goes on to show how it is possible to generate the following very complex sentence by combining seventeen propositions.

'He also noted that the cutback would apply only to the stock piling of weapons for an already bulging atomic arsenal and would have no effect on the overwhelming retaliatory strength of the SAC, of the Intercontinental missile force, or the Polaris missile fleet'.[19]

This is the procedure adopted by W. Schwab in the composition course: *Guide to Modern Grammar and Exposition*; having made the statement in the preface that 'in its presentation of grammar, this book is guided by modern linguistics, especially transformational grammar',[20] the author writes that the beginner 'should realize that even the most sophisticated sentences are built on or derived from a few basic types'.[21] On the basis of this he shows the systematic use of generalized transformations such as the following governing the introduction of relative constructions:

> 'Eliot dated a Thai girl,
> He had met her at the dean's reception,
> (Trel) He had met *whom* at the dean's reception,
> Whom he had met at the dean's reception.
> Eliot dated the Thai girl whom he had met at the dean's reception'.[22]

One finds similar examples of applications of transformational generative grammar in Nilsen's *A Transformational Approach to Composition* and H. R. Eschliman, R. C. Jones and T. R. Burkett's

Generative English Handbook but here the rules are given in a more abstract form. The following is an example:

INSERT	NP	Aux + VT	NP + m	(Adv)
	I	saw	the boy	yesterday
MATRIX	NP		VP	

	The boy	is the best choice				
RESULT NP	rel					
	that + m	NP	Aux + VT	(Adv)		VP
The boy	whom	I	saw	yesterday	is the best choice[23]

Unfortunately the results obtained with these textbooks are not available but it is possible to report the conclusions of an experiment going over two years in the teaching of composition with the aid of transformational generative grammar. The students in the experimental group obtained better results than those of a control group in two significant areas, (1) they wrote fewer ungrammatical sentences; (2) they wrote more elaborated constructions.[24]

At a more advanced level where more subtle problems of style arise as for example, the use of proforms in a paragraph, transformational generative grammar gives rise to more precise and explicit comments and corrections. This is pointed out by K. Schap: 'Transformational grammar finally takes discussion of language out of arbitrary realms and provides a vocabulary which makes a more concrete discussion of composition problems possible. Besides offering new insights about the nature of our language, transformational grammar enables us to explain precisely what makes good writing'.[25]

7. *Transformational generative grammar provides a system of rules permitting the generation of an infinite number of grammatical constructions.* In this it can contribute to the development among pupils of that creative aspect of language now coming to play a more and more important role in modern language learning. R. Hester underlines this particularly in his book *Teaching a Living Language.*

8. *From the time of its early descriptions of English, transformational generative grammar has shown very clearly that it possesses great generalizing power and is able to clarify underlying regularities up to now ignored by grammarians.* There is no doubt that in offering both to teacher and pupil more general rules in place of the traditional lists of exceptions and special cases, transformational generative grammar

is a very useful aid to teaching and learning. It is precisely this point which Rutherford takes up in the preface to his textbook: 'Although transformational theory as such does not tell us exactly how languages are learnt, it has nevertheless revealed the extent to which they have underlying regularity, deep and surface structure differences and universal similarity—discoveries which do have great relevance for language teaching'.[26] In points 9 and 10 below we return to these last two advantages pointed out by Rutherford. To illustrate the first, i.e. the discovery of underlying regularities and novel generalizations, we can simply refer to the treatment of *do* in Chomsky's *Syntactic Structures* (an example found in all of the textbooks of English already cited), or to the case of nominalizations in Lees' *Grammar of English Nominalizations*. This latter has been taken up among others in K. Croft's *English Noun Compounds* and in Earl Rand's work *Constructing Dialogs*. Indeed in French, where transformational generative descriptions are still too rare, one could probably improve teaching with a more precise knowledge of the ergative relations holding between different types of propositions and the rules which permit, via the introduction of one or two ergative subjects, the movement from intransitive constructions like the following:

(a) les documents brûlent

to the transitive proposition

(b) la secrétaire brûle les documents

and to the bitransitive proposition

(c) le directeur fait brûler les documents par la secrétaire.[27]

These rules which indicate a great generative power and generalizing power are not to be found in any school grammar.

9. *Transformational generative grammar makes a distinction between the surface structure and the deep structures of an utterance*, a distinction which we have already underlined in the preceding chapter as extremely important for language teaching. At the end of his article on the role of deep structures in the teaching of languages R. Jacobson writes 'This study seems to indicate that fast and adequate learning can only be achieved if deep structures are properly recognized and pedagogical procedures are so geared that the learner can derive from them the rules which he must internalize in order to become proficient in the target language. As a result the grammatical

structures presented in current textbooks of English as a foreign language must be re-examined in the light of present findings'.[28] We should make clear that applications in this area are still limited and hard to find. Recent textbooks like Rand's *Constructing Dialogs* and Rutherford's *Modern English* which make explicit reference to this distinction take considerable pains to avoid confusing in the same exercise utterances with different deep structures and to make clear the deep resemblances between utterances with heterogeneous surface structures. In other manuals, as for example *The Roberts English Series, A Linguistic Programme*, a return is made to this distinction between underlying and surface structures in order to highlight and explain certain syntactic ambiguities such as that of:

Ellen likes Scott as much as Sally (pages 406–408)

but this is still an isolated occurrence.

10. *Transformational generative grammar in a return to tradition admits the existence of linguistic universals and analogies between languages at the level of deep structure*, both areas which are of considerable importance for language teaching. In rejecting the structuralist conception of each language presenting an individual and singular structure, and in admitting with Chomsky that descriptions of all languages have the same general form and utilize the same type of rules (formal universals) and that they even present common categories and deep structures (substantive universals) the links between knowledge of the mother tongue and learning of a foreign language are shown in a new light. The mother tongue is no longer seen as forming (in the view of the authors of audio-visual courses) an annoying source of interference to be neutralized as quickly as possible; it is on the contrary from the outset a valuable and useful aid. Given that the teaching is conceived of rather differently from the manner in which it has been taught up to now, the pupil can acquire through his lessons in the mother tongue general information on the system and functioning of language which ought to make easier for him the learning of a foreign language. 'This task ought to be thought of as one in which in language teaching one introduces the pupil to those categories and concepts which, in the way they conform to general grammatical hypotheses, are valuable for all languages and applicable to all, and which in the learning and mastery of phenomena proper to each language at the level of lexis and of surface structure (syntax, morphology and phonetics) can be adequately explained as the realization of more general principles of linguistic structure in the

teaching of a particular language.'[29] The idea itself is not at all new, since, as Brekle points out, Sylvestre de Sacy made the identical point at the beginning of the nineteenth century in his book: *Principes de grammaire générale mis à la portée des enfans (sic) et propres à servir d'introduction à l'étude de toutes langues.* This new concept of mother tongue teaching as an initiation to general problems of language and as a preparation for foreign language learning is gaining more and more acceptance among language teachers nowadays: see for example the recent recommendation adopted by a symposium of the Council of Europe where the point is made that one should base the learning of the grammar of a second language on general knowledge of grammar acquired through the teaching of the mother tongue.[30]

11. *In postulating the existence of linguistic universals and of structures common to several languages, transformational generative grammar provides the basis for the necessary transfer from one language to another implicit in the areas of translation*[31] *and contrastive analysis important to language teaching.* In examining the advantages of generative grammar for Contrastive Analysis, G. Nickel commented at the Second International Congress of Applied Linguistics in Cambridge that: 'a further advantage is the conception of 'deep structure' and 'surface structure' in TG. In the light of this notion many structural differences between source and target language turn out to be merely superficial. A deep structure feature common to both languages may be manifested differently in the surface structure of the languages'.[32]

He gives as an example the following sentences:

> The accident killed many people
> Bei (durch den) dem Unfall wurden viele Menschen getötet

and

> This aircraft seats 100 people
> In diesem Flugzeug können 100 Personen Platz finden

where on the surface the structures appear quite different but which at deep structure level easily appear identical, particularly if one describes them in terms of Fillmore's Case Grammar, itself a variant of the transformational generative model.[33]

12. *Transformational generative grammar can characterize notions of grammaticality, ungrammaticality and degree of grammaticality which are indispensable for foreign language teaching particularly in the*

areas of evaluation (testing) and error analysis. It is worth remembering here that transformational generative grammar does not prescribe, in the way traditional grammar did, an absolute and arbitrary norm. It allows you to determine whether a particular sentence results from the correct application of a system of rules which one has chosen to teach (while being aware that there exist other systems and subsystems at other levels of language and dialects) and from the negative point of view it can indicate the number and type of violated or omitted rules. Using the model one can thus precisely describe the degree and nature of student error and be provided with an indispensable instrument for comprehension and correction of these errors. This in turn allows for a precise evaluation of the knowledge of the pupil and, as Pit Corder has very clearly shown, provides the data for a study of learning strategies: 'Errors are significant in three different ways, first to the teacher in that they tell him if he undertakes a systematic analysis, how far towards the goal the learner has progressed and consequently what remains for him to learn. Secondly they provide the researcher with evidence of how language is learned or acquired, what strategies or procedures the learner is employing in his discovery of the language. Thirdly (and in a sense this is the more important aspect) they are indispensable to the learner himself because we can regard the making of errors as a device the learner uses in order to learn'.[34]

13. *Transformational generative grammar can substantiate notions of deviation and style, thus providing a precise instrument for the stylistic analysis of literary texts.* In a very interesting article entitled *Generative Grammar and the Concept of Literary Style* R. Ohmann shows that traditional stylistic studies are at fault in being too impressionistic and subjective, or when they are precise, as for example with statistical studies, in being too partial and of little general significance. He puts forward rightly that this is due to the inadequacy of the concept of language on which these studies were based. In examining the contribution of Chomsky to stylistic studies, he writes: 'It is my contention that recent developments in generative grammar, particularly on the transformational model, promise first to clear away a good deal of the mist from stylistic theory and second to make possible a corresponding refinement in the practice of stylistic analysis'.[35] In examining the texts of four authors: Faulkner, Hemingway, James and Lawrence, he shows that it is possible to characterize their style in an explicit way according to the number and type of transformations which they use in the construction of their sentences.[36] Furthermore,

as J. P. Thorne has shown,[37] transformational generative grammar is an excellent instrument for the description of the characteristics of poetic style. He shows how poetry can be distinguished from prose by certain deviations from phonological, grammatical and semantic norms, or taking the problem from the other point of view, he shows how particular poets make use of their own phonological, grammatical and semantic rules. Transformational generative grammar allows for precise statements of deviations from some standard style by indicating omitted or violated rules. Finally, such analysis allows for the construction of the rule-system proper to any particular author.

14. *The most recent developments of transformational generative grammar in the areas of phonology and semantics provide novel and more systematic information which will come to play a more and more important role in language teaching.* Generative phonology, like generative grammar, reveals underlying similarities which up to now have escaped phonologists. Examples of this are the accent and stress rules for noun compounds in English proposed by Chomsky and Halle in their book *The Sound Pattern of English* and the liaison and elision rules for French given by Sanford Schane.[38] For the first time we have a systematic view of the links between the spoken code and its graphic transcription: this is particularly important for languages like French and English where structuralists constantly referred to the problems of aberrant phonology-orthography relations. Such information as this is extremely valuable both for the teaching of the systematic progression from one code to another or for the parallel study of both codes. As far as semantics is concerned, where at present the theory exists only in broad outline,[39] R. Wardhaugh has shown the importance of Fodor and Katz's information on the interpretation of sentences for the teaching of reading (reading comprehension): 'Comprehension requires far more than understanding the meanings of the individual words and then fusing these meanings by some mysterious process so that sense will result. It is this process, the fusion itself that requires a close examination. It has syntactic and semantic components about which the linguist can provide important information'.[40]

As for language teaching methodology, Chomsky has pointed out the gaps in Skinner's model of learning, but he has not yet been able to develop a valid model himself. In his defence one should point out that he has never made any claims that this theory was to provide the basis of a new methodology for language teaching. However, it is difficult to doubt that his ideas have orientated research into new directions and that they have contributed to the rehabilitation of certain pedagogic techniques too quickly condemned by structuralists. Chomsky's work has played an important role in determining these new interests and areas of research into language teaching, in particular the movement towards the study of learning processes, a point made clear by Pit Corder in 1967:[41] 'One effect has been perhaps to shift the emphasis away from preoccupation with *teaching* towards a study of *learning*'. In order to be clear about this, one only has to read the work of R. Hester *Teaching a Living Language*, which puts forward a language teaching methodology expressly referring to Chomsky's work even though such references often appear as a posteriori justifications.[42] The following comment of Lenard is a revealing one in this context: 'Above all a method, its techniques and materials must be *student-centered* as opposed to *text-centered*'.[43] Chomsky has contributed a great deal towards this shift of accent to an investigation of learning strategies as a first step towards working out a new language teaching methodology and the development of psycholinguistic research in an area nowadays occupying a central place in applied linguistics. As to pedagogic techniques, Chomsky has indirectly contributed to the revaluation of a number. For example:

(a) The value, as Corder suggests, of allowing pupils to make errors on the grounds that error-making constitutes an important element in their learning strategies: 'It is a way the learner has of testing his hypotheses about the nature of the language he is learning'.[44]

(b) The value of using ungrammatical examples to lead the pupil to test the limits of application of a rule and to acquire those generalizations which characterize his linguistic competence. As Robin Lakoff suggests: 'the teacher must give the learner a boost from making his own generalizations to learning how the native speaker understands and intuitively uses these sentences. This necessarily implies that it is essential to give the learner ungrammatical sentences, so that he can study these along with the grammatical ones to decide for himself what the difference is, so that when he is on his own and has to make a decision for himself, he can rely on his own new generalizing ability in this sphere to make the right generalization'.[45]

(c) The value of explanations in language learning, where, as Kandiah points out, transformational generative grammar 'restores intellectual activity to a position of respectability in the classroom'.[46]

(d) The priority accorded to free expression and creativity even at the expense of correction; a principle stressed by Hester: 'uncorrected

incorrectness is not to be feared as much as the banning of origi-
nality and the mistakes it entails'.[47]

As a more precise and more complete model, transformational
generative grammar appears to constitute an excellent basis for
renewal in language teaching pedagogy. However, the qualities which
we have picked out are open to argument and those attempts at
application that have taken place in the last ten years or so have, on
the whole, generally satisfied neither teachers nor linguists. Let us look
now at the objections to them and the most important gaps.

1. *Providing explicit descriptions forces transformational generative
grammars, particularly in more recent works, to utilize such an abstract
and complex formal apparatus that it cannot be made use of in teaching,
at least not at the early stages with children.* Perhaps teachers were
deceived by the simplicity of the early rewrite rules presented by
Chomsky in 1957 in *Syntactic Structures.* It appeared possible in
fact at this time to ask pupils to apply reasonably simple rules despite
their abstract presentation: e.g.

(1) Sentence→NP + VP

i.e. replace the symbol *Sentence* by the symbol NP (noun phrase)
followed by the symbol VP (verb phrase) and draw the corresponding
tree diagram:

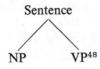

But transformational rules are more complex and more difficult to
apply. The following is for the passive transformation, itself one of
the most simple:

Structural analysis: NP — AUX — V — NP
Structural change: $X_1 - X_2 - X_3 - X_4 \rightarrow$
                       $X_4 - X_2 + be + en - X_3 - by + X_1$ [49]

i.e. from the tree representing the structure of the sentence one can
derive a new tree and a passive sentence by reordering the elements and
adding *be, en* and *by.*

Paul Roberts takes over Chomsky's rewrite and transformational
rules almost as they are into his programmed course *English Syntax,*
but again one can make the fair point of asking whether the gain in
precision which is thus obtained has not been bought at too high a

cost for the teacher: i.e. by the use of labels and very abstract symbols which are difficult to grasp and use for certain types of pupil.

In any case, what might have been thought possible in 1957 is no longer the case today. In most recent work where the metalanguage and linguistic units are extremely abstract and the rules extremely complex, it is no longer possible to use them for language teaching at any level at all.[50]

2. *Transformational generative grammar all too often leads in coursebooks to an empty formalism and to a too schematic representation which appears simplistic in the light of linguistic facts.* Even those manuals which claim to base themselves on transformational generative grammar only retain the most superficial aspects, least adapted to teaching, of the model—i.e. the metalanguage and the formalism, and ignore the more important aspects of, for example, Chomsky's theory, the notion of deep structures and the recognition of the existence of linguistic universals. J. D. Bowen and T. Moore remark: 'As there is more to mathematics than knowing the notation, so there is a great deal more to transformational theory than the clever juggling of formulas. In fact, overconcentration on formulaic abbreviations can obscure the underlying fundamental notions that the theory seeks to represent'.[51] In a similar way Robin Lakoff severely condemns Paul Roberts' attempts at application in *The Roberts English Series* or Owen Thomas's in his *Transformational Grammar and the Teacher of English*, 'These authors are not using transformational grammar: they are using only its hollow shell of formalism. Rather than teaching students to reason they seem to me to be teaching students to use new formulas. Instead of filling patterns of sentences— surface structures—students now have to learn patterns of abstractions—the rules themselves, and these rules are, without exception, fakes'.[52] In looking at a well-known example, i.e. the passive transformation in English as outlined by Chomsky in *Aspects of the Theory of Syntax*, Lakoff shows that it is inadequate and that as a result 'it is of no use as a pedagogical device, it does not enable students to reason better, nor does it make clearer generalizations that they need to know to use the passive as a native speaker does'.[53] What is important to retain from research work is not empty formalism but the overall conception of language, the heuristic methods which guide its investigation and the observations which researchers have made on this or that construction.

3. *Transformational generative grammar does not provide a linguistic or a methodological basis for structural exercises of a 'transformational'*

type. P. Rosenbaum notes clearly that: 'The rules in a transformational grammar are quite different from the rules countenanced by prescriptive linguistic descriptions and from the instructions for sentence building found in so many textbooks. Ongoing work in transformational grammar shows that it is incorrect to think of two sentences as being related by a transformational rule or set of rules which somehow converts one sentence into another'.[54] Clearly then it is necessary to distinguish two types of transformation; so-called naive transformations which convert one sentence into another, and Chomsky's transformations which convert abstract deep structures into surface structures which themselves can be subjected to morphophonological rules to generate the form of an oral or written sentence. This confusion probably stemmed from a too rapid reading of the first version of Chomsky's grammar where there was a distinction made between kernel sentences which correspond grosso modo to simple active declarative sentences: e.g.

> my mother cooks the dinner.

from which it is possible to produce by the use of optional transformations, negative active or interrogative structures as, for, example:

> my mother isn't cooking the dinner
> Is my mother cooking the dinner?
> Who's cooking the dinner?   etc.

These optional transformations appeared to provide the information needed for the development of structural exercises of a transformational kind because they made it possible for the pupil to move from a base structure to a derived structure. Since the formulation of these rules proved relatively complex for certain types of pupils, the idea of giving a rule in its explicit form was gradually abandoned and writers were content merely to illustrate sentence transformations with one or more models as, for example, in structural exercises for the language laboratory. In doing this, however, what was lost were precisely the advantages of a transformational rule, namely, the exact characterization of its domain of application. In replacing, for example, the transformational rule for the passive in French given by N. Ruwet:[55]

$$NP-Aux-Vtx-NP-X \rightarrow 4-2t + \text{être} + pp-3-\begin{Bmatrix} par \\ de \end{Bmatrix} + 1-5$$
$$1 2 3 4 5$$

with the examples

Jean a attendu Paul   Paul a été attendu par Jean

La police a arrêté le bandit   Le bandit a été arrêté par la police

from a teaching point of view, clearly, the abstract metalanguage has been done away with but at the cost of losing a good deal of information on the domain of application of the passive transformation. How for example, is one to know whether it would apply to the following utterances:

> La police a arrêté le bandit qui a dévalisé hier la banque principale→le bandit qui a dévalisé hier la banque principale a été arrêté par la police.
> Jean a attendu tout le matin→*Tout le matin a été attendu par Jean?

Examples of this kind do not enable the pupil to derive in a sufficiently general way rules which would ensure his correct usage of the passive.

The above comments have to do with the application of optional transformations to the development of structural exercises. Advocates of this type of application however, forget the other type of transformation, obligatory transformations, present in early Transformational Grammar, which are continued through to most recent versions of the model. Taking a very simple example from the description of the English Verb Phrase in *Syntactic Structures*, we see that in applying the replacement rules proposed by Chomsky and taken up in a number of school grammars already cited, it is possible among others to produce the following structure:

> the + cat + PAST + may + HAVE + pp + BE + ING + catch + a + mouse

from which with the help of transformation rules it is possible to derive the following:

> the + cat + may + PAST + HAVE + BE + pp + catch + ING + a + mouse

and, finally, applying morphophonological rules to produce the following English sentence:

> the cat might have been catching a mouse.

Obviously it is impossible to produce English sentences corresponding to each of the stages in this derivation. As a result, transformations do not convert a complete English sentence into another sentence but rather relate abstract deep structures to surface structures. The same is true for all transformations in the most recent descriptions with, however, the added complication that now transformations are applied to even more abstract deep structures, much more complex and even further removed from the output structures.

As far as language teaching methodology is concerned, it would be wrong to deduce from the fact that Chomsky makes use of transformational rules for language description that a language ought to be taught by means of transformational exercises. Anita Pincas makes this clear: 'The most serious misinterpretation is the belief that transformational grammar implies that language teaching should be by transformational drills'.[56]

4. *It is unlikely that grading in a language teaching course can be based on the progression of transformational rules.* This is so because as we have indicated above, transformational generative grammar is not to be seen as a system simply allowing all the sentences of a language to be constructed stage by stage from a small number of kernel sentences. As a consequence, it cannot indicate for the teacher a stock of basic utterances and what is more cannot provide any systematic progression from these basic utterances to more complex ones. Nor, on the other hand, is there anything which enables us to maintain at present that the system of rules elaborated by the linguist will for the description of a language constitute representation of the cognitive processes at work in the acquisition and use of a language. J. T. Lamendella has developed this argument at length both in an article entitled 'On the Irrelevance of Transformational Grammar to Second Language Pedagogy' and in his review of W. E. Rutherford's course *Modern English*, where he writes: 'We have no reason to believe that there is isomorphism or even any relationship whatsoever between the structures, categories and rules of any theory of description and the cognitive structures and processes involved when humans learn, store and use language'.[57] But it is important to make clear that Chomsky has himself contributed a good deal to the establishing and maintaining of this ambiguity ever since in *Syntactic Structures*[58] he first proposed the setting up of a system of rules permitting the characterization of all grammatical sentences of a language and then later in *Aspects of the Theory of Syntax*[59] made the suggestion that this system of rules constituted a model of native speaker's competence. One cannot exclude the possibility of an eventual extension of linguistic theory to a representation of these underlying

cognitive processes, but to do so would be to go beyond the resources of transformational generative grammar as presently understood.

5. *Transformational generative grammar only describes that competence, common to all native speakers of a language, for generating an infinity of grammatical sentences and leaves out of account the description of performance, the actual realization of competence in communicative situations.* Learning a foreign language implies, however, not only the acquisition of competence, i.e. the systematic rules of the foreign language, but also the acquisition of performance ability, i.e. the rules as applied to the reception and production of everyday speech. We know very little of the nature of these rules, and it is clear that even the best transformational generative descriptions only provide a part of the linguistic information necessary for the development of a language teaching course. Helbig suggests: 'One cannot seriously doubt the need for generative structures in language teaching but one must also be clear that these are structures of *langue* rather than necessarily the structures of *parole*; as such they do not correspond to those idiomatic structures essential for communication which need to be taught from the beginning of any teaching programme. This restriction is not an argument against generative theory, but it makes very clear the signification of applying such a theory to the teaching of foreign languages'.[60]

6. *More than the above, transformational generative grammar displays a very limited conception of linguistic competence.* In particular it neglects what Habermas[61] calls *communicative competence*; the basic need for which Wunderlich makes clear in the following terms: 'it would be absurd to elaborate an abstract capacity for the formation of speech utterances if one did not at the same time develop a capacity for communicating with the help of these utterances'.[62] In the same way in a classroom, it would be absurd to teach pupils to produce correct sentences in French if at the same time one was not also teaching them to use these sentences correctly for purposes of communicating in a variety of day-to-day situations. As Pit Corder points out, 'We are well aware of the rules for producing well formed sentences. These are the internal rules of the language. They are what we understand by the term code, but there are also rules which control the external relationship of utterances, which we can call rules of use'.[63] These rules are not provided by either any structuralist grammar or any transformational generative grammar. We cannot forget, therefore, that although the transformational model certainly presents a theory and a description of language superior to models which went

before, it is itself still far from providing teachers with all the linguistic information that they find necessary.

7. *Transformational generative grammar restricts itself in general to the description of sentences and as a result does not provide information on the structure of dialogues and of paragraphs.* Dialogue structure is necessary for the teaching of spoken performance and paragraph structure is needed for the teaching of writing as well as for the stylistic study of literary texts. As Wunderlich points out, 'there are only few publications where one can find a study of the conditions for the well-formedness of texts, e.g. thematic cohesion, consecutio temporum, pronominalization. There are even more important areas—the investigation of conversational structures and the study of teaching situations—what is needed here is the theoretical treatment of *texts* or rather chains of utterances which arise from alternating interlocutors'.[64] Wunderlich is underlining here the basic problem of *dialogues* which are both important for the definition of linguistic content in a course (the better one understands the linguistic structure of dialogues, in particular the relationship between questions and answers, the better one will be able to teach students to converse in a foreign language) and at the same time are fundamentally important for language teaching in general (since the dialogue between teacher and pupil is one of the principal instruments for such programmes).

8. *Transformational generative theory is in such a rapid state of flux that one hardly has time to apply one version of it to language teaching before that version is outdated and replaced by new modifications.* In effect, the theory has undergone such important changes from 1955–1965 that by the time that the first applications of the theory appeared in teaching materials,[65] they were already out of date. The situation has not improved since that time, from 1965 onwards, because the theory has developed along two different and concurrent paths; the lexicalist model represented among others by Chomsky and Jackendoff, and the transformationalist model represented in particular by McCawley, Lakoff and Ross. For the latter, the need for setting up traditional syntactic deep structures is no longer required: as an alternative, they propose deep *semantic* structures (generative semantics[66]) and as a metalanguage they generally employ the language of predicate logic. Despite what has been said on this point recently by Chomsky,[67] these two versions are not simply two different variants which differ only in their formulation. They reflect two basically different concepts of the structure of language. If one then makes

the point that neither of the theories is complete and both are open to a number of modifications, one can only see with difficulty how they could possibly be the basis for immediate application to teaching. What has to be the attitude of the teacher faced with such a situation? Clearly, he cannot hope to apply immediately to his teaching all the problems and partial solutions of linguists; their objectives are not his; but if he refuses to stick with tradition, what version of transformational generative grammar ought he to apply?

9. *Transformational generative descriptions of the major languages being taught are still too rare and too partial and often based on different versions of the theory.* The most complete descriptions relate to the first version of the model, since over the last ten years or so there has been a tendency among Chomsky's disciples to concentrate on points of detail in the theory rather than on extending our knowledge of the grammatical structure of particular languages. The aim has been one of testing the adequacy of new theoretical hypotheses rather than extending syntactic descriptions. These partial descriptions which are more orientated towards the theory than to possible applications, have little value for the teacher. One has to admit with W. F. Mackey that the development of a language teaching course ought to be able to begin from an overall unified description of the linguistic system of the language being taught. 'For a language teacher it is more useful to refer to a complete grammar than to a grammar which is scientifically coherent'.[68] Teachers are not in the position of having, with English as a possible exception, transformational generative descriptions which fulfil these conditions of coherence and completeness.

As far as the methodology of language teaching is concerned, we have already pointed out that Chomsky, although presenting severe criticisms of Skinner's learning model, has not himself developed a valid alternative. The informed teacher thus finds himself in an uncomfortable situation; conscious of the fact that the methodology realized in audio-visual methods and structuralist exercises is insufficient but not possessing valid alternatives. What is required now is rapid development in psycholinguistic research on second language acquisition.

NOTES

1 N. Chomsky: *The Logical Structure of Linguistic Theory*.

2 W. N. Francis: 'Revolution in Grammar'.

3   N. Chomsky: op. cit. pp. 38–39.

4   cf. E. Roulet: *Syntaxe de la proposition nucléaire en français parlé* pp. 83–84.

5   N. Chomsky: op. cit. p. 84 ff.

6   For more detailed and illustrated discussion of transformational analysis of modern French see: (1) N. Ruwet: *Introduction à la grammaire générative.* (2) E. Roulet: *Syntaxe de la proposition nucléaire en français parlé* (esp. pp. 81–165). (3) J. Nivette *Principes de grammaire générative.*

7   cf. E. Roulet op. cit. pp. 88–90.

8   N. Chomsky: 'Linguistic Theory'. p. 43.

9   P. Roberts: *English Syntax; Alternate Edition* p. 403.

10 P. Roberts: *English Sentences*: Preface p. viii.

11 J. W. Ney: 'Transformation Grammar in a Ryudai Classroom' p. 59.

12 M. Isacenko: 'Les structures syntaxiques fondamentales et leur enseignement' pp. 263 and 266.

13 E. Roulet: 'Quelques grammaires utiles à l'élaboration d'exercices structuraux pour le laboratoire de langues' p. 19.

14 W. Moulton: 'What is Structural Drill?' p. 13.

15 E. Rand: *Constructing Dialogs* p. vii.

16 T. Mueller, E. Mayer and H. Niedzielsky: *Handbook of French Structure, A systematic review* pp. 107 and 111.

17 T. Mueller et al.: op. cit. p. v.

18 K. W. Hunt: 'How little sentences grow into big ones' p. 176.

19 K. W. Hunt: op. cit. p. 185.

20 W. Schwab: *Guide to Modern Grammar and Exposition* p. xix.

21 W. Schwab: op. cit. p. 119.

22 W. Schwab: op. cit. p. 67.

23 H. R. Eschliman, R. C. Jones, T. R. Burkett: *Generative English Handbook* p. 41.

24 F. J. Zidonis: 'Generative Grammar: A Report on Research' p. 408.

25 K. Schap: 'Pronoun stress and the Composition Teacher' p. 172, cf. also J. Ross: 'Controlled writing, a transformational approach'.

26 W. E. Rutherford: *Modern English* p. ix.

27 cf. U. Egli and E. Roulet: *L'expression des relations d'ergativité et de transitivité dans une grammaire générative transformationelle du français.*

28 R. Jacobson: 'The rôle of deep structures in language teaching' pp. 159–160.

29 H. E. Brekle: *Allgemeine Grammatik und Sprachunterricht* p. 51.

30 Symposium of 16–20.11.1970 cf. also Y. Chalon: 'Reinforcement of the Mother Tongue in Adult Second-Language learning' in the *International Symposium of Applied Contrastive Linguistics*, Stuttgart 11–13. 10. 1971.

31 J. B. Walmsley: 'Transformation Theory and Translation'.

32   G. Nickel: 'Contrastive Linguistics and Foreign Language Teaching' p. 67.

33   G. Nickel: op. cit. p. 78. cf. also a more detailed treatment in: G. Rohdenburg 'Kasusgrammatik und kontrastive Analyse' in *PAKS Arbeitsbericht* 6: Stuttgart.

34   S. P. Corder: "The Significance of Learners' Errors' p. 167.

35   R. Ohmann: 'Generative Grammar and the Concept of Literary Style' p. 123.

36   Ibid pp. 128–136.

37   J. P. Thorne: 'Stylistics and Generative Grammars: Generative Grammar and Stylistic Analysis'.

38   S. Schane: *French Phonology and Morphology*.

39   J. J. Katz and J. A. Fodor: 'The Structure of a Semantic Theory.'

40   R. Wardhaugh: *Reading: A Linguistic Perspective* p. 66.

41   S. P. Corder: 'The Significance of Learners' Errors' p. 163.

42   cf. E. Roulet: Review of R. Hester: *Teaching a Living Language* in *Bulletin CILA* 13 pp. 73–75.

43   R. Hester op. cit. p. 47.

44   S. P. Corder 'The Significance of Learners' Errors' p. 167.

45   R. Lakoff: 'Transformational Grammar and Language Teaching' pp. 125–126.

46   T. Kandiah: 'The Transformational Challenge and the Teacher of English' p. 180.

47   R. Hester: 'Teaching a Living Language' p. 81.

48   N. Chomsky: *Syntactic Structures* pp. 26–27.

49   Ibid p. 112.

50   e.g. R. Jacobs and P. Rosenbaum: *Readings in English Transformational Grammar*.

51   J. D. Bowen and T. Moore: 'The Reflexive in English and Spanish: A Transformational Approach' p. 2.

52   R. Lakoff: 'Transformational Grammar and Language Teaching' p. 129.

53   Ibid p. 131.

54   P. Rosenbaum: 'On the role of linguistics in the teaching of English' pp. 474–475.

55   N. Ruwet: *Introduction à la grammaire générative* p. 363.

56   A Pincas: ' "Transformational", "Generative" and the EFL Teacher' p. 210.

57   J. T. Lamendella: Review of W. Rutherford: *Modern English* p. 150.

58   cf. p. 13.

59   cf. p. 4.

60   G. Helbig: 'Zur Anwendbarkeit moderner linguistischer Theorien im Fremdsprachenunterricht und zu den Beziehungen zwischen Sprach- und Lerntheorien' p. 302.

61   J. Habermas: *Einführende Bemerkungen zu einer Theorie der Kommunikativen Kompetenz*.

62   D. Wunderlich: *Die Rolle der Pragmatik in der Linguistik* p. 13, cf. also J. W. Oller: 'Transformational theory and pragmatics.'

63   S. P. Corder: 'Le rôle de l'analyse systématique des erreurs en linguistique appliquée' p. 11.

64   D. Wunderlich: 'Unterrichten als Dialog' p. 272.

65   P. Roberts: *English Sentences; English Syntax; The Roberts English Series.* O. Thomas: *Transformational Grammar and the Teacher of English.* W. O'Neil: *Kernels and Transformations.*

66   W. Abraham and R. I. Binnick: 'Syntax oder Semantik als erzeugende Komponenten eines Grammatikmodells?'

67   N. Chomsky: 'Some empirical issues in the theory of transformational grammar.'

68   W. F. Mackey: 'Applied Linguistics, its Meaning and Use' p. 13.

4

Linguistic Theories, Descriptions of a Language and Language Teaching

This rapid review of attempts at application over the last twenty years has clearly shown that though traditional grammar is insufficient to the task, modern grammatical theories and the descriptions which derive from them are far from furnishing complete solutions to teachers' problems. It would, however, be as well not to draw from this statement the bitter and premature conclusion that linguistics has no rôle to play in the renewal of language teaching methodology. The fact that linguistic research is incomplete and does not put forward panaceas for language teaching does not mean that it has nothing to contribute. G. Helbig makes the point that: 'At least the following is clear today: theory and linguistic description alone will not themselves lead to the development of practical realizations in language teaching but they do constitute an indispensable preamble to an efficient and optimal development of these practical realizations'.[1] This notwithstanding, it is still the case today, at least in Europe, that the majority of educationalists and teachers refuse squarely to be concerned with linguistic advice. As an argument for this non-involvement, they point to the lack of completeness of the descriptions and to the complexities and disparities among the rival theories. In almost the same breath, however, these same authorities and teachers quite happily admit that in order to teach modern mathematics it is necessary to have studied its theoretical bases. Why does the same argument not apply to language teaching? It is difficult to see how one can teach a particular language without a knowledge of the structure and functioning of language in general or of those mechanisms governing language acquisition. In a sense we are deceived by the fact that our language and, indeed, all aspects of language have been so well integrated into our daily existence from the beginning that they appear to us to be both familiar and simple. It is easy to admit naively that every human being, because he has learnt one language naturally and possesses it in a sense, spontaneously, has therefore learnt the system of this language, how it functions and how it is to be acquired. All one has to do is to ask questions of a number of teachers in order to be sure that under the influence of the normative teaching which they themselves have received, they are introduced to a host of false ideas on language problems. I see no way to deny the information contributed by contemporary linguistics. All attempts at revitalizing language teaching which ignore this particular fact sooner or later fail.

Rather than coming to hasty and often contradictory conclusions from the above that no changes can be made in language teaching, one can more profitably ask oneself if the problem of applying theories and linguistic descriptions to language teaching, particularly to grammar teaching, has not been very frequently posed in the wrong way. On closer examination, in fact, attempts at application during the last twenty years or so suffer from three major drawbacks.

(1) They imply the possibility of direct transfer of the results of linguistic research to language teaching.

(2) The term 'application' is ambiguous and embraces a wide range of differing results, dependent on what it is one is borrowing from the theory or description in question: lists of structures or rules, analytical procedures, a metalanguage or, merely, a general view of the nature of language.

(3) Whatever one applies, what is presupposed is a unidirectional relation between theory, description and teaching, along the following lines:

$$
\begin{array}{c}
\hline
\text{Theory} \\
\hline
\Downarrow \\
\hline
\text{Description} \\
\hline
\Downarrow \\
\hline
\text{Teaching} \qquad [2] \\
\hline
\end{array}
$$

On the first point, it is clearly naive to believe that there can possibly exist a direct link between linguistic research and language teaching. As Arndt points out: 'in no case can one necessarily draw from the appearance of a new scientific grammar Gs of a language L definitive conclusions for a new ideal pedagogic grammar Gp. There is no direct relationship between Gs and Gp'.[3] This does not come at all as a surprise given that linguistics and language teaching are different disciplines with different goals, different methods and metalanguages.[4] Certain problems studied by linguists hold no interest at all for teachers; similarly certain aspects of language teaching have no relevance for linguistics.

On the second point, in order to avoid all kinds of confusions and misunderstandings, what must be precisely made clear each time one speaks about the possible applications of linguistics to language teaching, is exactly what one is applying. Answering that kind of question enables one to exercise much more differentiated judgement on the possible interest and value of different applications. The attempts referred to in preceding chapters derive from the following range of views on 'applying' linguistics:

(a) *Linguistic theory provides the teacher with information on the structure and functioning of the language system in general which may play a role in the way he defines the goals, content and presentation of his language teaching course.* This is what Spolsky calls 'implications' in order to make a distinction from direct 'applications'.[5] This is also de Saussure's distinction between 'syntagmatic' and 'paradigmatic' relations,[6] or the way Chomsky's distinction between surface and deep structure is reflected in the content and presentation of a number of recent coursebooks.[7] In the same way the return to a 'universal grammar' with its recognition of linguistic universals may offer fundamental modification to the goals of mother tongue teaching particularly in the way of foregrounding general principles governing the structure and functioning of a language.[8] This mode of application has the great advantage of being independent of generally inadequate or unsatisfactory descriptions of particular languages. It is also the point of view which least suffers today from counter-arguments since the linguist can propose basic information without prejudging the manner in which it will be used by teachers. As a mode of application it is likely, in our view, to influence particularly strongly changes in language teaching methodology.

(b) *Linguistic theory provides the teacher with a metalanguage: e.g. formal universals like the different types of rules in a generative grammar (replacement rules, transformational rules, etc.) and substantive universals like the categories Noun Phrase, Verb Phrase, etc., or syntactic features like ± Animate, ± Stative which he can use in the presentation of a language teaching course.*[9] However, what was possible for a long time when linguists, as for example in traditional grammar, used everyday language enriched with a number of technical terms as a metalanguage now appears no longer possible given that the origins of the linguists' 'language' lie in logic and mathematics. The linguist and the language teacher today have two quite different goals to be able to make equally successful use of the same metalanguage.

(c) *Directly or indirectly the views of linguistic theory on language acquisition do influence language teaching methodology; particularly the way in which language courses are presented.* Sol Saporta comments: 'Strangely enough the impact of the descriptive linguistics of the '40s and '50s on language teaching was primarily on the form and only incidentally on the content of pedagogical grammars'.[10] This remark explains a good deal of the false direction of the last twenty years in attempts at modernizing language teaching methodology. Given that the linguist could contribute a great deal when it was a matter of choosing and describing the material to be taught, it was the psycholinguist or the psychologists of language learning or, indeed, the teacher, who was the appropriate person for defining methods of presentation adequate for the selected material.

(d) *A language description necessarily makes the teacher more aware of the language structures to be taught, thus improving the quality of the linguistic content of his language teaching course.* This type of application together with (a) above are certainly the most frequently met with and the most fruitful. Remembering at this point the novel contribution of structuralist grammar to the study of the morphology of the spoken language (in particular in French and English) and that of transformational generative grammar in the area of syntax (nominalizations, causative constructions), we have gained information which, without prejudging the manner in which the teacher is to present it to the pupils, nevertheless has given teachers a much more complete and precise knowledge of the system of the language they are teaching.

(e) *A linguistic description provides the language teacher with a range of units (phonemes, morphemes, tagmemes, etc.) as well as a list of structures or a system of rules for the given language, which he can introduce in a course without adaptation.* What distinguishes this mode of application from the one that went before, of course, is that here the teacher is taking over linguistic information and teaching it in the same form and way as it has been presented by the linguist. Again, here, the same objection to that already formulated under (b) above will occur; i.e. the differences between the objectives and metalanguages of linguists and teachers.

(f) *Further, a linguistic description provides an ordered system of rules which can be translated in teaching terms into a graded sequence of material.* We have already shown in the preceding chapter that it would be premature, to say the least, to accept the hypothesis of a correspondence between the rules of a generative grammar and the cognitive processes governing language learning,[11] particularly in the light of the common assumption that individuals follow often very different learning strategies. There cannot then exist any ideal progression which defines the function of a system of a language. What we have are numerous variations according to the aptitudes and needs of individual learners, and this is a problem rather for psychologists of language learning and psycholinguists than for linguists.

(g) *Linguists provide neither theory nor language description but simply analytical techniques* (e.g. minimal pair contrasts in phonology or the setting-up of substitution tables in a tagmemic analysis) which can be made use of by the teacher on his own for solving problems badly handled in the coursebooks or, alternatively, in the classroom with his pupils, as a method of making them aware of the structures of the language under study. This is an interesting way of approaching the problem of application but all too often teachers are happy with simply borrowing an attractive idea from a particular theory or method such as the idea of transformation or that of the substitution slot, without in any way being involved in the theoretical or methodological framework on which these notions are based. One ought not, therefore, to talk about the application of linguistics in this trivial sense, as has often been the case with so-called 'transformational' exercises which claim to be based on transformational generative grammar but which in fact do nothing but reproduce a pedagogic technique well established before Chomsky.

Clearly, this list of methods of application is not at all exhaustive; it does allow us, however, to suggest that the problem of the possibilities of application is much more various than it at first appears and to bring forward a variety of judgements on the different attempts at application of the last few years. Nevertheless, and this is the third point which we raised at the beginning of this chapter, whatever the method of application, it still will reflect a wrong conception of the relationship between linguistics and language teaching. In all the methods so far, what is presupposed is a unidirectional relationship between linguistic theory, description and language teaching. From grammatical theory, descriptions of particular languages are derived, descriptions which themselves then serve as the basis for the writing of language teaching courses. As a result, what one ends up with is a number of unfortunate misinterpretations or misunderstandings between linguists and language teachers of which the following is an example. One of the most frequent arguments advanced for condemn- ing attempts at applying linguistics to language teaching lies in the incomplete character of the linguistic descriptions of those languages most frequently taught.[12] In looking at recent anthologies of studies on the transformational analysis of English,[13] teachers in particular have been led to conclude that the syntactic descriptions of English are so fragmentary, disparate, and limited to the study of marginal cases that they could never achieve any usefulness for the teaching of English itself. From this they have prematurely concluded that transformational generative grammar has nothing to contribute to English teaching. To follow this argument is to forget that the studies in question were not intended to provide us with a more complete and more systematic description of the English language but rather to test the adequacy of the transformational generative model, to dis- cover its weaknesses and to propose possible modifications. Pit Corder has characterized particularly well this new orientation. 'Describing natural languages is of course an activity in which the purely theoretical linguist engages but his objectives are those of testing the validity of his theory and not those of providing informa- tion or instruction to the non-linguist. The theoretical linguist in his role of linguist is concerned with the nature of human language, not with producing a comprehensive account of any particular language. It is therefore not a matter of surprise that during the last half century or so during which we have seen the ever sharpening distinction between theoretical linguistics and descriptive linguistics, there has been a notable absence of comprehensive scholarly descriptions of well-known languages derived from modern theoretical principles'.[14] In other words the descriptions of English mentioned above neither formed for their authors an end in themselves nor a collection of materials able to be variously applied to other disciplines, be it to language teaching or to machine translation, as the diagram illustrates:

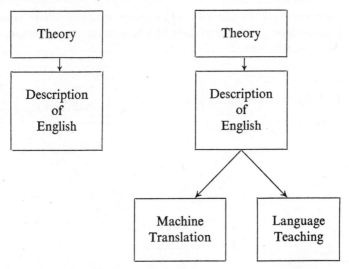

In fact, such articles were orientated towards seeing the relationship in the following way:

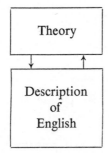

and had as their objective the testing of the adequacy of the theory. One is now in a much better position to understand the interest they evoked for linguists even though they were fragmentary studies of marginal cases. What is more we can now understand why they frequently held little value for teaching purposes. One ought to be very careful not to judge the question of the possible application of transformational generative grammar on the simple basis of these test descriptions.

There is, then, no one-way relationship between linguistics—either theory or description—and language teaching. The latter, in fact, has much to contribute to the former in posing precise problems and in offering the possibility of verifying empirically these theories or descriptions. Thus, the relationships between the three domains ought to look more like the following:

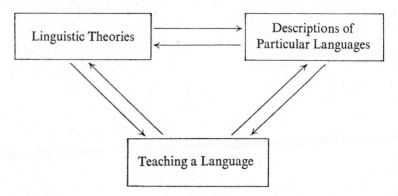

If one then goes on to make the point that linguistics is not the only variable in language teaching and that it is necessary to take account of language learning theories, one arrives at Spolsky's model:

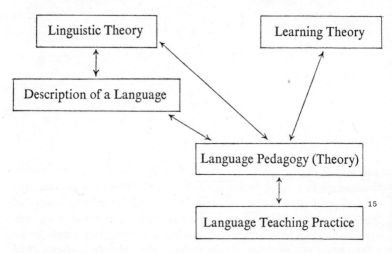

This scheme makes clear what has been missing in previous attempts at applying linguistics to language teaching.

In starting out from the results of linguistic research, which has been the usual practice since Bloomfield, and asking of it what it could contribute to language teaching, the risk run is that of tackling the problem from the wrong end and of believing, as did American structuralists, that linguistics controlled all conceivable inputs to language teaching. It is only when one begins from the circumstances and aims of language learning that linguistics takes its proper place among those disciplines concerned with renewing language teaching methodology, i.e. sociolinguistics, psycholinguistics, the psychology of language learning, pedagogy, etc., and we can make a choice of the most adequate among the available theories and descriptions.

The principal aim of teaching modern languages is to permit individuals to communicate with others in the diverse personal and professional situations of daily living. Realizing this objective involves accepting three conditions often neglected by those who define them.

Firstly, possessing a language as an instrument of communication is not simply a matter of being capable of constructing and understanding grammatical sentences. It is also a question of knowing how to use these sentences in given linguistic and non-linguistic contexts. In other words, we need to know, on the one hand, how to combine these sentences into larger communicative units, e.g. texts and dialogues, and on the other hand, to produce and use appropriate utterances in certain communicative situations in relation to particular aims, the role and status of our interlocutors, the topic of the conversation and the channel of transmission employed, to cite only the most important factors.

Secondly, communicating with interlocutors is not simply a question of transmitting information or posing questions on the objects and events which surround us ('He begins work at eight o'clock', 'The bathroom is between the two bedrooms'). Besides this referential, cognitive or denotative function (to use Jakobson's terminology[16]), other functions of language come in and can in fact dominate everyday talk. One of the interlocutors may concentrate principally on asserting himself, expressing his attitude, his feelings, his judgements of others or of the topic of the conversation. This can be called the expressive or emotive function. He may, however, seek to cause someone else to act (the conative function) or may simply wish to talk for the purpose of establishing or maintaining contacts with other people (the phatic function). Imagine the situation of a student coming into a foreign country; what counts most for him is establishing and maintaining contacts with native speakers so as to be able to participate as much as possible in the life of the community. It may frequently turn out that these contacts or indeed the communication itself is blocked or unsuccessful as a result of simple misunderstanding of expressive, phatic or conative traits of the dialogue, even though the referential content of the message is perfectly transmitted. Knowing a language as an instrument of communication is thus not simply being in command of the referential function but also of the expressive, phatic, conative and poetic functions as well.

Thirdly, and as a corollary, communicating satisfactorily in a linguistic community is not simply a matter of knowing a pure, homogeneous and monolithic language; one needs to be able at least to understand and if possible to use different varieties of the language used in the particular community. As Jakobson writes,[17] 'For a whole speech community, for all native speakers there exists a unity of language; but this global code represents in communication a system of reciprocal subcodes. Each language embraces a number of simultaneous systems of which each one is characterized by a different function'. This is a very important fact, since in communicating with others, the choice of variety of language used is very closely related to the present and future affective, professional and social relationships, of the interlocutors as well as the content of the conversation. Knowing a language as an instrument of communication is to be able to understand its principal subcodes and to know how to use them in appropriate situations.

We can take as an illustration a concrete example well known today among sociolinguists, but which has never been systematically treated in language teaching courses; the use of expressions of address and salutation. In a great number of languages, the speaker has a choice between two pronouns in speaking to his interlocutor; *tu* and *vous* in French, *ty* and *vy* in Russian, *du* and *Sie* in German, *du* and *ir* in Yiddish, etc. At the same time the speaker generally has a choice between different modes of address: a first name (John) a surname (Smith) the title plus surname (Mr. Smith) and different expressions of greeting (*Hello, Good-day, Good-day Mr. Smith*, etc.). Now these choices in communication often have a much more important meaning than the purely referential content of messages because they give to each of the interlocutors precise information, particularly in the opening stages of a new relationship, on the attitude and the feelings of the other interlocutor to themselves. They may, indeed, exercise a determining influence on the way in which this relationship develops. An important example here is *tutoiement* in French. For speakers expressing themselves in their mother tongue, the use of these expressions as a function of the affective and social status of the interlocutor is so automatic and natural that it presents no problem. This is not the case with a foreigner, however, for even if the use of these terms is governed by probably universal traits, the actual forms of use are different from one community to another. A misunderstanding of the rules of use which are required in a certain community both for comprehension and expression may have considerably disturbing consequences for the social life of a foreigner. These consequences can, in fact, be more serious than fundamental repetitive errors in grammar, vocabulary and pronunciation. Now most language teaching courses do not treat these particular problems and language teachers generally have only a vague and imprecise awareness of the rules of use of these particular expressions.

We have now sufficiently described the demands on the use of language as an instrument for communication to re-examine the contribution of linguistics to language teaching pedagogy. The principal linguistic theories from de Saussure to Chomsky, which have been applied to problems of language teaching, have all failed to provide information on the use of language as an instrument of communication. What they have done in fact is:

(a) to describe only the system and not the use of the language: Candlin makes the comment: 'Useful though such an input from several linguistic grammars may be, the question begged is clearly that if a pedagogical grammar is at the basis of language teaching materials, and if such materials have as their aim to lead the learner to "knowledge" of the second language, then they and the pedagogical grammar must be as concerned with rules of language use as they are with rules of grammaticality and well-formedness of sentences'.[18]

(b) to treat only the structure of the sentence and neglect communicative units such as *text* and *dialogue*. As Widdowson writes: 'If we are to teach language in use we have to shift our attention from sentences in isolation to the manner in which they combine in text on the one hand, and to the manner in which they are used to perform communicative acts in discourse on the other'.[19] For this purpose what is required is a text grammar which will include rules for the combination of sentences in a text and a discourse grammar which will present the rules of use for utterances in communicative acts.

(c) to study systematically only the referential function of language, neglecting other functions. Frake notes: 'To ask appropriately for a drink among the Subanun it is not enough to know how to construct a grammatical utterance in Subanun translatable in English as a request for a drink. Rendering such an utterance might elicit praise for one's fluency in Subanun, but it would probably not get a drink. Our stranger requires more than a grammar and lexicon. He needs what Hymes has called an ethnography of speaking, a specification of what kinds of things to say in what message forms to what kinds of people in what kinds of situations'.[20] We shall return later to this contribution of Hymes.

(d) to study only one variety of the language, itself considered as homogeneous and representative and to pay no attention to other varieties which are part of the verbal repertoire of the linguistic community.

This distinction between the two approaches: a theory of language system and a theory of language use, reflects the distinction between *Langue* and *Parole* drawn by de Saussure in his *Course in General Linguistics*. *Langue* is a code, a system of social conventions, common to all the members of a speech community. *Parole*, however, is the individual actualization of this code in daily communication. From this has grown the notion that linguistics ought to study as a priority and perhaps exclusively, the system of *langue*, only turning to the study of *parole* at some future date. In this way de Saussure's distinction resulted in a rapid development of the study of the system of language but this at the same time had the effect of unfortunately directing linguists away from the study of language use. De Saussure in fact, as Ducrot[21] pertinently remarked, 'equates linguistic activity and individual initiative' thus relegating all study of human activity to the study of parole, as a secondary issue. Hence the neglect of studies of language use, communicative units like texts and dialogues, and the different functions for which language may be used.

Given that many aspects of our use of language are not dependent on our individual initiatives but seem to be governed by social conventions quite as systematic as the code of language, it is for us to make these the object of just as rigorous a study.

Classical transformational generative theory in terms of the work of Chomsky, Katz and Halle, though constituting a considerable contribution to linguistic description and theory, nevertheless remains a theory of language seen as a formal system. What it does is to characterize linguistic competence in a restricted sense, i.e. the capacity to construct correct grammatical sentences independent of all linguistic or situational context, maintaining the fiction of a monolithic, pure and homogeneous language. As Gumperz writes: 'Despite the increase in the scope of linguistic descriptions, the new theory continues to make sharp distinctions between grammars and the social context in which utterances are used'.[22] Relegated to the area of performance as they were previously to the area of *parole*, are very diverse elements not at all distinguished in terms of psychological and individual factors of social conventions. In brief, classical transformational generative theory considerably reinforces our knowledge of the system of the language but gives us no information on the use of language and different subcodes as instruments of communication for different sociolinguistic functions. As soon as one begins to apply such a theory to a concrete area of activity like language teaching, it rapidly becomes clear that, despite the possibilities it offered for considerable elaboration in its own limited terms, the theory in its present form is untenable. This limitation to the analysis of linguistic form contributes also to the relative lack of success seen in attempts to apply linguistics to language teaching. Linguistics from de Saussure to Chomsky has not been thought of in a way likely to provide the necessary information for the teaching of languages as instruments of communication.

Rather than starting from the contribution of most well known linguistic theories and asking of them what they can bring to language teaching pedagogy, it would in fact be better to begin from the demands of teaching languages as instruments of communication and on that basis look at other approaches to language. Gumperz posed the question quite clearly in 1965, 'It seems necessary, at least for the purpose of applied linguistics, to reopen the question of the relationship between linguistics and social facts. More specifically, the question arises given a grammatical analysis of the languages involved of what additional information the sociolinguist can provide in order to enable the language teacher to give his students the skills they need to communicate effectively in a new society.'[23]

Alongside the research discussed so far, then, there have always existed views, which, although remaining peripheral to linguistics until quite recently, are now seen to have concerns very much closer to those of applied linguistics. What we refer to is what Hymes calls today the 'ethnography of communication'.

Ever since 1935, Firth rejected the traditional conception of a monolithic and homogeneous language: 'There is no such thing as "une langue unie" and there has never been'.[24] He observed that we all play different social roles according to different situations, and that each role has corresponding to it a certain variety of language. At the same time he made the point that *parole* was not a 'boundless chaos' and that conversation was much more structured than one would generally believe. In fact, according to Firth, we are not at all free to say what we want since our language activity is governed to a large degree by conventions which bind us to our particular roles and situations. Malinowsky in 1936 suggested that one should abandon the distinction between *langue* and *parole* and affirm that the principal object of linguistic study was living speech in a context of situation: 'The present reviewer, like most anthropologists, would plead for the empirical approach to linguistics, placing living speech in its actual context of situation as the main object of linguistic study'.[25]

These few references suffice to show that at the period of the early attempts to apply linguistics to language teaching many linguists already maintained the possibility and need for a systematic study of different varieties of language and use. What one regrets is that these linguists have not yet been sufficiently heard by applied linguists and teachers.

It was during the 1960s that under the impetus of Hymes and other sociolinguists and under the label of 'ethnography of communication' or 'ethnography of speaking', the study of the uses of different varieties of language was established as an area of research within linguistics which has since enjoyed very rapid development. Hymes has defined the object of this study in these terms: 'This is a question of what a child internalizes about speaking beyond rules of grammar and a dictionary while becoming a full fledged member of its speech community. Or it is a question of what a foreigner must learn about a group's verbal behaviour in order to participate appropriately and effectively in its activities. The ethnography of speaking is concerned with situations and uses, the patterns and functions of speaking as an activity in its own right'.[26] This definition shows straight away how much the preoccupations of researchers in the area of ethnography of communication are in agreement with teachers' needs. What characterizes this particular approach is its overall examination of the verbal activities of a linguistic community and its study of all the varieties of language used in such a community, i.e. its verbal repertoire, rather than a limitation to the description of one or more of these codes or subcodes. Verbal exchanges within the community are analysed in communicative situations (hunting, eating, courtship), which can then be divided into communicative events which are more limited and essentially verbal (conversation) and are themselves formed of speech acts (commending, questioning, joking, etc.).[27]

Each speech act or communicative act is analysed in its turn into a certain number of component elements; labelled by present research as: *form and content of the message*, *setting* (either geographical, temporal or psychological), *participants* (speaker, hearer, addressee), *verbal purposes, modalities* (i.e. tone and mode in which the act is performed), *channel of communication* (oral, written, telegraphic), *variety of language used* (dialects, registers, etc.), *norms of interaction* (expression in a deep voice, silent listening, etc.), *norms of interpretation* (as a function of the belief system of the community) and *genres* (poems, stories, proverbs, etc.[28]).

The purpose of these investigations is to be able to establish rules of speech or communication emphasizing relationships between the different components of communicative acts and thus to provide language use with a formal description.[29]

As an example, a number of interesting results have already been obtained in the description of expressions for personal address and reference. The point of their importance to the study of communicative competence has been made earlier. Brown and Ford,[30] and Brown and Gilman[31] have isolated the different variables governing the use of these expressions of address in English, and Ervin-Tripp has recently shown[32] that it is possible to formalize rules to account for their use.

There is no doubt that such an approach can contribute precise information to the teaching of languages seen as instruments of communication. Unfortunately, the theory itself only exists in outline form, the analytic models are programmatic and the descriptions themselves rare or partial. One should make the point, however, that applied linguists and teachers need not necessarily wait for theoretical research results before beginning their own work along these lines.

The problem is in fact less grave than it might otherwise appear because one can begin redefining the objectives and content of language teaching materials in the light of the principles of the ethnography of communication while awaiting the availability of systematic description.

In the light of these probabilities Gorosch has proposed beginning the task of defining the content of a language teaching course by a systematic analysis of sociolinguistic situations in a given society.[33] Such an approach might include the following stages:

(A) Analysis of sociolinguistic situations

(i) inventory of the current sociolinguistic situations (daily communication, industry, commerce, administration, research, etc.) by teams of linguists, sociolinguists and specialists in the particular disciplines under study.

(ii) systematic analysis of the situations and their linguistic components (syntactic, lexical and phonological structures) and extralinguistic components (sociocultural context).

(iii) determination of the nature and degree of knowledge required (oral and written comprehension and performance) in order to control sociolinguistically particular individual situations.

(B) Definition of language teaching objectives

(i) Long term objectives: linguistic knowledge required to achieve control of one or more linguistic situations given.

(ii) Short term objectives: linguistic knowledge required for different stages in the acquisition of this control.

(C) Definition of the content of the language teaching course

Definition of the linguistic content (phonological, syntactic and lexical structures) and the sociocultural content of the different parts of the course: development of oral comprehension, oral expression, written comprehension and written expression.

Such a scheme as this has two important advantages. On the one hand, it highlights the necessity of defining language teaching objectives precisely. This is extremely valuable at a time when researchers and language teachers have not provided these teaching objectives either for mother tongue work or for foreign language teaching and where the content of language teaching courses has remained traditionally unchanged. Secondly, it bases the definition of these objectives and language teaching course contents on the systematic analysis of sociolinguistic situations.

Notwithstanding these advantages, Gorosch's scheme has two major faults: in defining his method of presenting the material to be taught, he does not underline the necessity of knowing what are appropriate learning strategies for different categories of individuals or groups. No one believes any longer that there is a single 'most efficient' way of teaching languages as was believed a little naively by the writers and teachers of the early audio-lingual courses and audio-visual methods. Each individual according to his age and personal characteristics, his surroundings, his previous training, spontaneously adopts the learning strategy which suits him best. For that reason alone it is a mistake to seek to impose on an adult an unchanging inductive audio-lingual learning programme[34] if he has had experience of a variety of different learning strategies. Clearly, the choice of grading, sequencing and method is not determined by the description of the language to be taught or by the analysis of a linguistic situation alone. Contreras makes the comment: 'A pedagogical grammar is based on a scientific grammar but includes something else in addition. The particular organization of materials in a pedagogical grammar for instance, presumably derives from a theory of language learning and not from a scientific grammar'.[35] In other words, to the analysis of sociolinguistic situations has to be added a *study of learning strategies* with the following set of stages:

(A) *Knowledge of language learning mechanisms*
(a) for the language being acquired (first language, second language, etc.).
(b) for the situation in which the learning takes place.
(c) for the intellectual capacity, age and cultural level of the individuals or groups involved.
(d) for the different skills to be acquired in the long term (written and oral comprehension and production).

(B) *Definition of the selection and presentation of linguistic facts* most suited to promote rapid development of this learning mechanism in individuals or groups within particular situations and in relation to the sociolinguistic control of one or more given linguistic situations.

(C) *Choice of pedagogical techniques* (types of dialogue between teacher and pupil, teaching machine and pupil, or pupil-to-pupil, types of exercise) and *choice of media* (coursebook, audio tape, programmed learning, etc.), selecting among these those most appropriate for passing information to the individual or the group at the appropriate moment in the language learning programme.

Completed in this way, Gorosch's original scheme allows the material which is to be learnt to be defined, as well as the best way of teaching it, but there still remain considerable obstacles at the level of defining objectives in language teaching. According to Gorosch, analysing the most frequent sociolinguistic situations ought to make us aware of the needs of our society in terms of people with diverse linguistic competences and therefore to define the language teaching objectives in terms of the function of these needs. At this point the serious question arises whether it should be the aim of our educational system to adapt individuals to the needs of society. Indeed, even if one gives an affirmative answer to this question, one still has to admit that the needs of modern society change so rapidly that there are grave risks of inappropriate adaptation if one gives a too highly specialized linguistic training to all individuals. If what is needed is to grasp and accept all the implications of shifting language training centred on the teacher and the method to a language learning pedagogy centred on the pupil, what is required is to take a great deal of notice of the motivations and needs of individuals and groups as they develop spontaneously in the framework of their individual experiences or of their lives within this society.[36] Whether for children or adults, at all stages of language learning, a number of factors of environment and personal taste tend to orientate the motivations and needs of the learner towards this or that sociolinguistic situation, and as a result towards the mastery of this or that area of language use. It is for this reason that instead of imposing on all those who learn a language a single globally valid content and method of learning, it would be better to allow each individual spontaneously to lean towards the control of this or that sociolinguistic situation using the particular learning strategies and media best appropriate to him. This naturally presupposes the abandoning of linear and monolithic language teaching courses and implies the creation of a considerable quantity of teaching material allied to the use of very subtle techniques. This is so since all of the units of content defined in terms of their function in sociolinguistic situations ought to be available to the learner in random order, to be selected according to the motivations of the individual or the group, and to be presented in different forms via different media so as to be amenable to different types of learning strategy. This in turn also implies the disappearance of the language teaching class in its traditional form where a group of students follow exactly the same programme: it further implies the replacement of traditional examinations by a continuous process of self-evaluation. Fortunately, both of these areas of innovation are at present gradually being introduced in other teaching areas. In the final analysis what we are aiming for here is a continuing programme of education— éducation permanente.[37]

Given this general position one can now attempt to state more precisely the place of theories and grammatical descriptions (or more generally the place of linguistics) among the principal disciplines of interest to language teaching. One can do this by completing Spolsky's diagram in the following way:

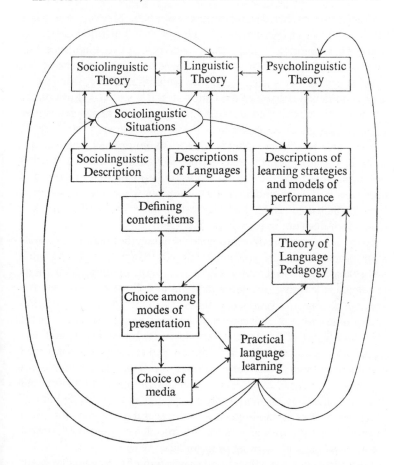

This scheme, which is not intended to present a complete model of the interrelationship between all the disciplines concerned in language teaching, nevertheless does allow for putting theories and grammatical descriptions in their precise place; as such, it makes clearer the intention of linguistics in language teaching. It also indicates the erroneousness of those attempts at revitalizing language learning which do not take account of the contribution of linguistics, psycholinguistics and sociolinguistics and which seek to remain at the simple level of practical teaching, and in particular, the attempt of those applied linguists and language teachers who are happy simply to administer prescriptions for the use of language laboratories and audio-visual methods.

For the researcher, this plan makes clear the necessity of a rapid breaking down of the divisions which generally separate the areas of general or theoretical linguistics from descriptive linguistics and applied linguistics. Research into language teaching and learning can only progress seriously within an interdisciplinary framework. Unfortunately too many general linguists today still look down on the work of descriptive and applied linguistics; too many descriptive linguists produce monographs without making any reference to theory, and finally and above all, too many applied linguists are quite ignorant of general or descriptive linguistics. Thus, as Culioli has often repeated, the distinction established between theory and application is false and injurious since one cannot conceive of a theory which does not have an application nor conceive of an application which does not in turn draw on a theory.

In the same way, the divisions which separate the areas of linguistics from psycholinguistics, sociolinguistics and language teaching must be broken down. No serious contribution to the updating of methods of language learning can be made without a consensus between the areas of theory and practice in these disciplines. For collaboration to continue and be effective, research and teaching centres must be set up where teams of linguists, psycholinguists, sociolinguists and language teachers can work on common projects and be concerned equally with theory, description and application. Too often, centres of applied linguistics are too cut off both from linguistic theory and practical pedagogy, as well as from research in other disciplines of psycholinguistics, sociolinguistics and general pedagogy for them to provide satisfactory answers to the problems posed by desirable changes in language learning programmes.

For the teacher, the content and conclusion of this particular book are perhaps deceiving since far more problems are posed than resolved, but linguists and psychologists have for too long led language teachers astray in presenting them with 'scientific' definitions of simple or false concepts. The problem of making basic changes in language learning programmes is extremely complex and one will not arrive at the answer by oversimplifying whatever the contributions are that come from other disciplines. General and Applied Linguistics are such recent disciplines that it is not surprising that they are not yet at the point where they can pose definitive answers to problems. All they can do is indicate them and this is what we have tried to do here, but the incompleteness of the research does not absolve the language teacher from the need to inform himself and to be able to understand

and follow those important shifts of interest both in the theory and practice of language learning.

NOTES

1 G. Helbig: "Zur Anwendbarkeit moderner linguistischer Theorien im Fremdsprachenunterricht und zu den Beziehungen zwischen Sprach- und Lerntheorien' p. 290.

2 cf. the scheme proposed by J. P. Vinay in *Enseignement et apprentissage d'une langue seconde* p. 700.

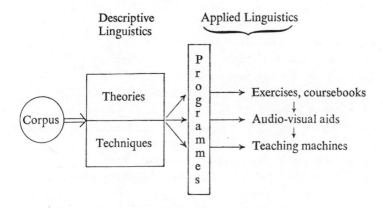

3 H. Arndt: 'Wissenschaftliche Grammatik und pädagogische Grammatik' p. 67.

4 cf. W. Motsch: 'Sprachwissenschaft und Sprachunterricht' p. 20.

5 B. Spolsky: 'Linguistics and Language Pedagogy: Applications or Implications?'

6 cf. J. Guenot: *Clefs pour les langues vivantes:* Chapter III 'L'usine structuraliste' pp. 63–79.

7 cf. the preface to W. E. Rutherford: *Modern English* p. ix.

8 cf. H. E. Brekle: 'Allgemeine Grammatik und Schulunterricht'.

9 cf. P. Roberts: *English Syntax.*

10 S. Saporta: 'Applied Linguistics and Generative Grammar' p. 82.

11 cf. J. T. Lamendella: 'On the irrelevance of Transformational Grammar to Language Pedagogy'.

12 cf. W. J. Mackey: 'Applied Linguistics, its meaning and use' p. 13.

13 D. A. Reibel, S. A. Schane (eds) *Modern Studies in English, Readings in Transformational Grammar* or R. Jacobs and P. Rosenbaum (eds) *Readings in English Transformational Grammar.*

14 S. P. Corder: 'Applied Linguistics' p. 16.

15   B. Spolsky: 'Linguistics and Language Pedagogy—Applications or Implications?' p. 147.

16   R. Jakobson: 'Linguistics and Poetics—Closing statement' in T. Sebeok (ed) *Style in Language*.

17   Ibid.

18   C. N. Candlin: 'The Status of pedagogical grammars' p. 58.

19   H. Widdowson: 'Directions in the teaching of discourse' p. 69.

20   C. Frake: 'How to ask for a drink in Subanun' pp. 87–88.

21   O. Ducrot: 'De Saussure à la philosophie du langage' p. 11.

22   J. Gumperz: 'Linguistic repertoires, grammars and second language learning' p. 82.

23   J. Gumperz op. cit. p. 84.

24   J. R. Firth: 'The techniques of semantics' p. 67.

25   B. Malinowski: Review of M. M. Lewis *Infant Speech* p. 63.

26   D. Hymes: 'The ethnography of speaking' p. 101.

27   cf. D. Hymes: 'Models of interaction and social life'.

28   D. Hymes: op. cit. pp. 58–65.

29   W. Labov: 'The study of language in its social context'. S. Ervin-Tripp: 'On sociolinguistic rules: alternation and cooccurrence'.

30   R. Brown and M. Ford: 'Address in American English'.

31   R. Brown and A. Gilman: 'The pronouns of power and solidarity'.

32   S. Ervin-Tripp: op. cit.

33   M. Gorosch: 'Goal oriented Modern Language Teaching' cf. also papers from the Skepparholmen Conference (19–24.10.1970).

34   *Voix et Images de France*, for example.

35   H. Contreras: 'Transformational Grammar and Language Teaching' p. 11.

36   cf. W. E. Lambert, R. C. Gardner, R. Olton and K. Tunstall: 'A Study of the roles of attitudes and motivation in Second-Language Learning.'

37   cf. research under the sponsorship of the *Comité de l'éducation extra-scolaire et développement culturel* of the Council of Europe esp. the *Rüschlikon Symposium* (3–7.5.1971) on 'Le contenu linguistique, les moyens d'évaluation et leur interaction dans l'enseignement et l'apprentissage des langues vivantes comme partie de l'éducation des adultes', and the *St. Wolfgang Symposium* (17–28.6.1973) on 'A Unit/Credit system for Modern Languages in Adult Education', particularly John Trim's reports: *Draft Outline* and *Consolidated Report*.

Bibliography

Note: Only the works quoted in the text are listed in sections A and C. Section B comprises a more important list of works and articles dealing with the possible applications of the theories and grammatical descriptions to teaching languages. This list cannot claim to be totally comprehensive but it may aid the interested reader in further study of this area, for which as yet there is no comprehensive bibliography.

A. General linguistics, descriptive linguistics, sociolinguistics

Abraham, Werner and Binnick, R. I.'Syntax oder Semantik als erzeugende Komponenten eines Grammatikmodells?' in *Linguistische Berichte* **4**, 1969, 1–28.

Arnauld and Lancelot. *Grammaire générale et raisonnée*, Paris, Républications Paulet, 1969.

Bloomfield, Leonard. *Language*, New York, Holt, Rinehart and Winston, 1933.

Bowen, J. Donald and Moore, Terence. 'The Reflexive in English and Spanish: A Transformational Approach', in *English Teaching Forum* **7/4**, 1969, 2–11.

Brown, R. W. and Ford, M. 'Address in American English', in *JASP* **62**, 1961, 375–385.

Brown, R. W. and Gilman, A. 'The Pronouns of Power and Solidarity', in Sebeok, T. A. (ed.): *Style in Language*, New York, Wiley, 1962, 253–276.

Chevalier, Jean-Claude. 'Eléments pour une description du groupe nominal: Les prédéterminants du substantif', in *Le Français moderne* **34**, 1966. 241–253.

Chomsky, Noam. *Aspects of the Theory of Syntax*, Cambridge, MIT Press, 1965.

Chomsky, Noam. *Cartesian Linguistics*, New York, Harper and Row, 1966.

Chomsky, Noam. *Language and Mind*, New York, Harcourt, Brace and World, 1968.

Chomsky, Noam. *Some Empirical Issues in the Theory of Transformational Grammar*, 1970, mimeo.

Chomsky, Noam. *Syntactic Structures*, The Hague, Mouton, 1957.

Chomsky, Noam. *The Logical Structure of Linguistic Theory*, Cambridge, MIT, 1955, mimeo.

Chomsky, Noam. *Topics in the Theory of Generative Grammar*, The Hague, Mouton, 1966.

Chomsky, Noam and Halle, Morris. *The Sound Pattern of English*, New York, Harper and Row, 1968.

Damourette, J. and Pichon, E. *Des mots à la pensée, Essai de grammaire de la langue française*, Paris, d'Artrey, 1911–1930.

Dubois, Jean. *Grammaire structurale du français, I Nom et pronom, II Le verbe*, Paris, Larousse, 1966–1967.

Ducrot, O. 'De Saussure à la philosophie du langage', Preface to Searle J. R.: *Les actes de langage*, Paris, Hermann, 1972.

Egli, Urs and Roulet, Eddy. *L'expression des relations d'ergativité et de transitivité dans une grammaire générative transformationelle du français*, Berne, Institut de linguistique de l'Université, Arbeitspapier 3, 1971.

Ervin-Tripp, S. 'On Sociolinguistic Rules: Alternation and Cooccurrence', in Gumperz, J. J. and Hymes, D. (eds.).: *Directions in Sociolinguistics*, New York, Holt, Rinehart and Winston, 1972, 213–250.

Fillmore, Charles J. 'The Case for Case', in Bach, E. and Harms, R. T. (eds.), *Universals in Linguistic Theory*, New York, Holt, Rinehart and Winston, 1968, 1–88.

Firth, J. R. 'The Techniques of Semantics', in *Transactions of the Philological Society*, 1935, 36–72.

Fishman, J. A. *Sociolinguistique*, Bruxelles, Labor, Paris, Nathan, 1971.

Frake, C. O. 'How to Ask for a Drink in Subanun', in *American Anthropologist* **66/6**, 1964, 127–132.

Glinz, H. *Die innere Form des Deutschen*, Berne, 1952.

Gougenheim, G., Michea, R., Rivenc, P. and Sauvageot, A. *L'élaboration du français fondamental (1er degré), Etude sur l'établissement d'un vocabulaire et d'une grammaire de base*, Paris, Didier, rev. ed. 1964.

Guillaume, G. *Le problème de l'article et sa solution dans la langue française*, Paris, Hachette, 1919.

Habermas, J. *Einführende Bemerkungen zu einer Theorie der kommunikativen Kompetenz*, 1970, roneo.

Hall, Jr., Robert A. *French*, Baltimore, Waverly Press, 1948.

Halliday, M. A. K. 'Categories of the Theory of Grammar', in *Word* **17**, 1961, 241–292.

Harris, Zellig S. *Methods in Structural Linguistics*, Chicago, The University of Chicago Press, 1951.

Heringer, Hans-Jürgen. 'Einige Ergebnisse und Probleme des Dependenzgrammatik', in *Der Deutschunterricht* **22/4**, 1970, 42, 98.

Hill, A. A. *Introduction to Linguistic Structures, From Sound to Sentence in English*, New York, Harcourt, Brace and World, 1958.

Hymes, D. 'Models of Interaction of Language and Social Life', in Gumperz, J. J. and Hymes, D. (eds.), *Directions in Sociolinguistics*, New York, Holt, Rinehart and Winston, 1972, 35—71.

Hymes, D. 'The Ethnography of Speaking', in Gladwyn, T. and Sturtevant, W. C. (eds.). *Anthropology and Human Behaviour*, Washington, Anthropological Society, 1962, 13–53.

Jakobson, R. 'Linguistique et poétique', in *Essais de linguistique générale*, Paris, Minuit, 1963, 209–248.

Katz, Jerrold J. and Fodor, Jerry A. 'The Structure of a Semantic Theory', in *Language* **39**, 1963, 170–210.

Labov, W. 'The Study of Language in its Social Context', in *Studium Generale* **23**, 1970, 30–87.

Lamb, Sidney. *Outline of Stratificational Grammar*, Washington, Georgetown University Press, 1966.

Lees, Robert R. *The Grammar of English Nominalizations*, The Hague, Mouton, 1966.

Leonard, S. A. *Current English Usage*, Chicago, Inland Press, 1932.

Longacre, Robert E. *Grammar Discovery Procedures*, The Hague, Mouton, 1964.

Lyons, John. *Introduction to Theoretical Linguistics*, Cambridge, University Press, 1968.

Lyons, John. *New Horizons in Linguistics*, Harmondsworth, Penguin Books, 1970.

Malinowski, B. *Review of M. M. Lewis, Infant Speech*, in *Nature* **140**, 1937, 172–173.

Marckwardt, A. H. and Walcott, F. *Facts about Current English Usage*, New York, Appleton-Century-Crofts, 1938.

Martinet, A. *Eléments de linguistique générale*, Paris, Colin, 1960.

Mitterand, Henri. 'Observations sur les prédéterminants du nom', in *Etudes de linguistique appliquée* **2**, 1963, 126–134.

Nivette, Joos. *Principes de grammaire générative*, Brussels, Labor, Paris, Nathan, 1970.

Palmer, Harold E. *The Scientific Study and Teaching of Languages*, New York, World Book Company, 1917; new edition London, Oxford University Press, 1968.

Pike, Kenneth L. *Language in Relation to a Unified Theory of the Structure of Human Behaviour*, Glendale, Summer Institute of Linguistics, 1954–1960; new edition The Hague, Mouton, 1967.

Postal, Paul. *Constituent Structure, a Study of Contemporary Models of Syntactic Description*, Bloomington, Indiana University, 1964.

Roulet, Eddy. *Syntaxe de la proposition nucléaire en français parlé, étude tagmémique et transformationnelle*, Brussels, AIMAV, 1969.

Ruwet, Nicolas. *Introduction à la grammaire générative*, Paris, Plon, 1967.

Ruwet, Nicolas. 'Note sur la syntaxe du pronom en et d'autres sujets apparentés', in *Langue française* **6**, 1970, 70–83.

Saussure, Ferdinand de. *Cours de linguistique générale*, Paris, Payot, 1916.

Schane, Sanford A. *French Phonology and Morphology*, Cambridge, MIT Press, 1968.

Schane, Sanford A. 'L'élision et la liaison en français', in *Langage* **8**, 1967, 37–59.

Tesnière, L. *Eléments de syntaxe structurale*, Paris, Klincksieck, 1959.

Weisgerber, L. *Grundzüge der inhaltsbezogenen Grammatik*.

Wells, R. S. 'Immediate Constituents', in *Language* **23**, 1947, 81–117.

Wilmet, Marc. *Gustave Guillaume et son école linguistique*, Brussels, Labor, Paris, Nathan, 1972.

Wunderlich, D. 'Die Rolle der Pragmatik in der Linguistik', in *Der Deutschunterricht* **22/4**, 1970, 5–41.

B.   Applications of grammatical models to language teaching

Abraham, Werner. 'Neue Wege der angewandten Sprachwissenschaft— Erkennungs- und Erzeugungsgrammatik', in *Muttersprache*, 1970, 181–191.

Abraham, Werner. 'Syntaktische Einfachstrukturen zur Förderung des Sprachgefühls im Englischen', in *Erziehung und Unterricht* **119/1**, 1969, 25–35.

Abraham, Werner. 'Zur Taxonomie der «Angewandten Sprachwissenschaften»', in *Bulletin CILA* **11**, 1970, 6–18.

Achtenhagen, Frank. *Didaktik des fremdsprachlichen Unterrichts, Grundlagen und Probleme einer Fachdidaktik*, Weinheim, Julius Beltz, 1969.

Achtenhagen, Frank. 'Didaktik des fremdsprachlichen Unterrichts und Linguistik-Überlegungen zu den Möglichkeiten und der Notwendigkeit einer Kooperation', in *Linguistische Berichte* **4**, 1969, 80–85.

Adamczewski, Henri. 'La grammaire générative transformationnelle et l'enseignement des langues vivantes', in *Bulletin pédagogique IUT*, mai 1969, 1–37.

Alexander, L. G. 'The New Grammarian and the Language Teacher', in *English Language Teaching* **24/1**, 1969, 5–11.

Allen, Harold B. *Readings in Applied English Linguistics*, New York, Appleton-Century-Crofts, (2nd ed.), 1964.

Angewandte Linguistik—Französisch, Kiel, Arbeitsgruppe für angewandte Linguistik, Französisch, 1970.

Anisfeld, Moshe. 'Psycholinguistic Perspectives on Language Learning'. Valdman A. (ed.), *Trends in Language Teaching*, New York, McGraw-Hill, 1966, 107–119.

Arndt, Horst. 'Wissenschaftliche Grammatik und pädagogische Grammatik', in *Neusprachliche Mitteilungen* **2**, 1969, 65–76.

Arnold, Werner. 'Die Stellung der Grammatik in der Didaktik des Französischunterrichts an Unter- und Mittelstufe', in *Der fremdsprachliche Unterricht* **2**, 1967, 23–34.

Aurbach, J., Cook, PhJ., Kaplan, R. T. and Tufte, V. J. *Transformational Grammar: A Guide for Teachers*, Rockville (Maryland), English Language Series, 1968.

Bartsch, W. 'Behandlung der Grammatik im Fortgeschrittenenunterricht', in *Deutschunterricht für Ausländer* **18/3–4**, 1968, 115–123.

Bausch, Karl-Heinz. *The Teaching of German in German Schools and Current Trends in Linguistics in German Universities*, Freiburg, Institut für deutsche Sprache, 1970, mimeo.

Belasco, S. 'Les structures grammaticales orales', in *Le français dans le monde* **41**, 1966, 37–46.

Besse, Henri. 'Grammaire structurale et exercices structuraux', in *Voix et images du CREDIF* **6**, 1970, 2–5.

Bolinger, Dwight. 'A Grammar for Grammars: The Contrastive Structures of English and Spanish', in *Romance Philology* **21**, 1967, 186–212.

Bosco, F. J. and Di Pietro, R. J. 'Instructional Strategies: Their Psychological and Linguistic Bases', in *IRAL* **8**, 1970, 1–19.

Berkle, H. E. 'Allgemeine Grammatik und Schulunterricht', in *Linguistik und Didaktik* **1**, 1970, 48–55.

Brown, T. Grant. 'In Defense of Pattern Practice', in *Language Learning* **19**, 1969, 191–203.

Bünting, Karl Dieter. 'Wissenschaftliche und pädagogische Grammatik (Sprachwissenschaft und Sprachlehre),' in *Linguistische Berichte* **5**, 1970, 73–82.

Capelle, Guy. 'Les apports de la linguistique moderne à l'enseignement des langues', in *Cahiers pédagogiques* **47**, 1964, 5–10.

Candlin, C. 'The Status of Pedagogical Grammars', in Corder, S. P. and Roulet, E. (eds.).: *Theoretical Linguistic Models in Applied Linguistics*, Brussels, AIMAV and Paris, Didier, 1973, 55–64.

Carroll, John B. 'The Contributions of Psychological Theory and Educational Research to the Teaching of Foreign Languages', in Valdman, A. (ed.). *Trends in Language Teaching*, New York, McGraw-Hill, 1966, 93–106.

Carstensen, Broder. 'Die alte und die neue Grammatik im Fremdsprachenunterricht in unserer Zeit: Berichte aus Universität und Schule', in *Sonderheft zur Praxis des neusprachlichen Unterrichts*, 1965, 40–52.

Carstensen, Broder. *Die «neue» Grammatik und ihre praktische Anwendung im Englischen, Forschungsbericht*, Frankfurt, Moritz Diesterweg, 1966.

Chastain, Kenneth. 'The Audio-lingual Habit Theory versus the Cognitive Code-learning Theory: Some Theoretical Considerations', in *IRAL* **7**, 1969, 97–106.

Chevalier, Jean-Claude. 'Grammaire, linguistique et enseignement des langues', in *Langues modernes* **64**, 1970, 33–48.

Chevalier, Jean-Claude. 'La linguistique moderne et les expériences pédagogiques,' in *Neusprachliche Mitteilungen* **3**, 1970, 129–130.

Chevalier, Jean-Claude. 'L'enseignement de la langue française et la linguistique moderne', in *Pour l'enseignement moderne du français contemporain*, Paris, Larousse, 1968, 17–20.

Chevalier, Jean-Claude. 'Quelle grammaire enseigner?', in *Le français dans le monde* **55**, 1968, 21–25.

Chomsky, Noam. Review of B. F. Skinner, *Verbal Behavior*, in *Language* **35**, 1959, 26–58.

Chomsky, Noam. 'Linguistic Theory', in *Northeast Conference Reports, Language Teaching: Broader Contexts*, Menasha Wisconsin, 1966, 43–49.

Clark, John. 'Competence and Performance: The Missing Links', in *Audio-visual Language Journal* **7/1**, 1969, 31–36.

Combettes, B., Demarolle, P., Copeaux, J. and Fresson, J. *L'analyse de la phrase, contribution à une application pédagogique des théories linguistiques modernes*, Nancy C.R.D.P., 1970.

Contreras, Helen. 'Transformational Grammar and Language Teaching', in *Revista de linguistica aplicada* 5/1, 1967, 6–17.

Cook, Vivian, J. 'Freedom and Control in Language Teaching Materials', 1970, mimeo, B.A.A.L. Conference Papers, Child Language Survey, University of York, York, England.

Corder, S. P. and Roulet, E. (eds.). *Linguistic Insights in Applied Linguistics*, Brussels, AIMAV and Paris, Didier, 1974.

Corder, S. P. and Roulet, E. (eds.). *Theoretical Linguistic Models in Applied Linguistics*, Brussels, AIMAV and Paris, Didier, 1973.

Corder, S. P. 'Idiosyncratic Dialects and Error Analysis' in *IRAL* 9, 1971, 147–159.

Corder, S. P. 'Le rôle de l'analyse systématique des erreurs en linguistique appliquée', in *Bulletin CILA* 14, 1971, 6–15.

Corder, S. P. 'The Significance of Learners' Errors', in *IRAL* 5, 1967, 161–170.

Corder, S. P. *Applied Linguistics: Various Interpretations and Practices*, Strasbourg, Conseil de l'Europe, 1971, mimeo.

Corder, S. P. *Introducing Applied Linguistics*, Harmondsworth, Penguin, 1973.

Crystal, David. 'New Perspectives for Language Study, 1. Stylistics', in *English Language Teaching* 24, 1970, 99–106; 2, Semiotics, ibid. 209–215.

Crystal, David. 'Stylistics, Fluency and Language Teaching', in *Interdisciplinary Approaches to Language*, London, Centre for Information on Language Teaching, 1971, 34–53.

Csecsy, Madeleine. *De la linguistique à la pédagogie: le verbe français*, Paris, Hachette/Larousse, 1968.

David, Jean. 'Les exercices de constitution progressive de texte: essai d'utilisation pédagogique de la notion de transformation', in *Bulletin pédagogique IUT* 11, 1970, 60–72.

Debyser, F. 'L'enseignement du français langue étrangère au niveau 2', in *Le français dans le monde* 73, 1970, 6–14.

Delattre, P. 'La notion de structure et son utilité', in *Le français dans le monde* 41, 1966, 7–11.

Denninghaus, F. 'Der Einfluss der Linguistik auf die Didaktik und Methodik des Fremdsprachenunterrichts', in *Neusprachliche Mitteilungen* 3, 1970, 130–131.

Denninghaus, F. 'Die wechselseitigen Einflüsse zwischen der Linguistik und dem Fremdsprachenunterricht', in *Praxis des neusprachlichen Unterrichts* 18/1, 1971, 31–40.

Diack, Hubert. 'A Re-examination of Grammar', in *The Use of English* 7/4, 1956, 251–255; reprinted in Wilson, G., *A Linguistics Reader*, New York, Harper and Row, 1967, 152–156.

Dingwall, William Orr. 'Transformational Generative Grammar and Contrastive Analysis', in *Language Learning* 14, 1964, 147–160.

Di Pietro, Robert J. 'Contrastive Analysis and the Notions of Deep and Surface Grammar', in *Monograph Series on Languages and Linguistics* 21, 1968, 65–80.

Dykema, Karl. 'Progress in Grammar', in *College English* 14/2, 1952, 93–100; reprinted Wilson, G. *A Linguistics Reader*, New York, Harper and Row, 1967, 158–165.

Eberhard, Marc. 'L'utilisation de la théorie de la grammaire générative et transformationnelle en pédagogie des langues vivantes', in *Bulletin pédagogique IUT* **15**, 1971, 23–33.

Engels, L. K. 'The Function of Grammar in the Teaching of English as a Second Language', in *ITL* **10**, 1970, 11–23.

Erlinger, Hans-Dieter. *Sprachwissenschaft und Schulgrammatik, Strukturen und Ergebnisse von 1900 bis zur Gegenwart*, Düsseldorf, Pädagogischer Verlag Schwann, 1969.

Filipovic, Rudolf. 'Contrastive Trends in Applied Linguistics', in *Contact* **14**, 1970, 13–17.

Flämig, W. 'Probleme und Tendenzen der Schulgrammatik', in *Der Deutschunterricht* **6**, 1966, 340ff.

Foster, David William. 'A Model for Drilling some Points of Grammar', in *Language Learning* **15**, 1965, 7–15.

Francis, W. Nelson. 'Revolution in Grammar', in *Quarterly Journal of Speech* **40**, 1954, 299–312; reprinted in Allen, H. B., *Readings in Applied English Linguistics*, New York, Appleton-Century-Crofts (2nd ed.), 1964.

Frey, Emm. 'Lage und Möglichkeiten der Schul- und Volksgrammatik', in *Der Deutschunterricht* **18**/5, 1966, 5–46.

Galisson, Robert. *L'apprentissage systématique du vocabulaire*, Paris, Hachette/Larousse, 1970.

Galisson, Robert. *Inventaire thématique et syntagmatique du français fondamental*, Paris, Hachette/Larousse, 1971.

Gefen, Raphael. 'Let's Transform Generations and Categorize Theories', in *Language Learning* **16**, 1966, 71–76.

Gefen, Raphael. '«Sentence Patterns» in the Light of Language Theories and Classroom Needs', in *IRAL* **5**, 1967, 185–192.

Girard, D. 'Vers une conception scientifique de l'enseignement des langues', in *Les langues modernes* **62**/6, 1968, 39–47.

Gladney, Frank Y. 'Applicable Linguistics for Language Teachers', in *Illinois Journal of Education* **57**/6, 1965, 27–32.

Gleason, Jr., H. A. *Linguistics and English Grammar*, New York, Holt, Rinehart and Winston, 1965.

Gorosch, Max. 'Goal-oriented Modern Language Teaching', in *Cibal* **1**, 1970, 67–83.

'Grammar in Language Teaching', in *Modern Languages* **49**, 1968, 108–115.

Griffe, G. 'Grammaire structurale du français moderne', in *Bulletin de la société Binet Simon* **69**, 1969, 122–134.

Guenot, Jean. *Clefs pour les langues vivantes*, Paris, Seghers, 1964.

Gumperz, J. J. 'Linguistic Repertoires, Grammars and Second Language Instruction', in *Monograph Series on Languages and Linguistics* **18**, 1965, 81–90.

Gutnecht, Christoph and Kerner, Peter. *Systematisierte Strukturmodelle des Englischen, Lernpsychologische und methodologische Grundfragen zur Pattern-Grammatik*, Hamburg, H. Buske, 1969.

Haddock, N. 'Practical Applications and Limitations of Generative Grammar', in *Audio-visual Language Journal* **8**, 1970, 89–91.

Hall, Jr., Robert A. 'Contrastive Grammar and Textbook Structure', in *Monograph Series on Languages and Linguistics* **21**, 1968, 175–183.

Halliday, M. A. K., McIntosh, Angus and Strevens, Peter. *The Linguistic Sciences and Language Teaching*, London, Longman, 1964.

Harsh, Wayne. 'Three Approaches: Traditional Grammar, Descriptive Linguistics, Generative Grammar', in *English Teaching Forum* 6/4, 1968, 2–10.

Hartmann, W. 'Unterrichtsbeispiele zur Arbeit mit der generativen Grammatik im Deutschunterricht', in *Wirkendes Wort* 5, 1969, 289–310.

Heddesheimer, C. 'Théorie grammaticale et enseignement de la grammaire', in *Mélanges CRAPEL* 1970, Nancy.

Helbig, Gerhard. 'Die Bedeutung syntaktischer Modelle für den Fremdsprachenunterricht', in *Deutsch als Fremdsprache* 4, 1967, 195–204, 259–267.

Helbig, Gerhard. 'Graduierung der Grammatikalität und Leistungsbewertung im Sprachunterricht', in *Deutsch als Fremdsprache* 8, 1971, 1–12.

Helbig, Gerhard. 'Zur Applikation moderner linguistischer Theorien im Fremdsprachenunterricht und zu den Beziehungen zwischen Sprach- und Lerntheorien', in *Deutsch als Fremdsprache* 1, 1969, 15–27; reprinted as: 'Zur Anwendbarkeit . . .' in *Sprache im technischen Zeitalter* 32, 1969, 287–305.

Hensel, Gerhard. 'Vom Recht auf sprachwissenschaftliche Einsicht im neusprachlichen Unterricht', in *Der fremdsprachliche Unterricht* 3, 1967, 22–32.

Herndon, Jeanne H. *A Survey of Modern Grammars*, New York, Holt, Rinehart and Winston, 1970.

Hester, Ralph (ed.). *Teaching a Living Language*, New York, Harper and Row, 1970.

Hill, Archibald, A. 'Language Analysis and Language Teaching', in *Modern Language Journal* 40, 1956, 335–345.

Hill, Archibald A. *The Promise and Limitations of the Newest Type of Grammatical Analysis*, Cincinnati, University, 1966.

Hoppe, Alfred. 'Aufbau einer Sprachunterrichtsmethodik auf der «kommunikativen Grammatik»', in *Der Deutschunterricht* 21/4, 73–97.

Hughes, John P. *Linguistics and Language Teaching*, New York, Random House, 1968.

Hundsnurscher, F. et al. *TSG Transformationelle Schulgrammatik*, Göppingen, Verlag Kümmerle, 1970.

Hunt, Kellog W. 'How Little Sentences Grow into Big Ones', in Lester, Mark, *Readings in Applied Transformational Grammar*, New York, Holt, Rinehart and Winston, 1970, 170–186.

Hunt, Kellog W. 'Recent Measures in Syntactic Development', in *Elementary English* 43, 1966, 732–739; reprinted in Lester, Mark, *Readings in Applied Transformational Grammar*, New York, Holt, Rinehart and Winston, 1970, 182–200.

Hwang, Juck-ryoon. 'Current Theories of Language Learning and Teaching', in *English Teaching Forum* 8/2, 1970, 26–29.

Ianni, Lawrence. 'An Answer to Doubts about the Usefulness of the New Grammar', in *The English Journal* 53, 1964, 597–602.

Isacenko, M. 'Les structures syntaxiques fondamentales et leur enseignement', in *Actes du premier colloque international de linguistique appliquée*, Nancy, 1966, 252–266.

Jacobs, Roderick A. and Rosenbaum, Peter S. *Readings in English Transformational Grammar*, Waltham, Ginn, 1970.

Jacobson, Rudolfo. 'The Role of Deep Structures in Language Learning', in *Language Learning* 16, 1966, 153–160.

Jakobovits, Leon A. 'Implications of Recent Psycholinguistic Developments for the Teaching of a Second Language', in *Language Learning* 18, 1968, 89–109.

James, Carl. 'Deeper Contrastive Study', in *IRAL* 7, 1969, 83–95.

James, Carl. 'The Applied Linguistics of Pedagogic Dialogues', in *Language Learning* 20, 1970, 45–54.

Jean, Georges. 'La linguistique moderne et l'enseignement du français langue élémentaire', in *Le français d'aujourd'hui* 2, 1968, 10–16.

Johnson, Francis C. 'The Failure of the Discipline of Linguistics in Language Teaching', in *Language Learning* 19, 1969, 235–244.

'Journée d'étude sur l'enseignement de la grammaire', in *Revue des langues vivantes* 36, 1970, 453–544.

Kadler, Eric H. *Linguistics and Teaching Foreign Languages*, New York, Van Nostrand Reinhold, 1970.

Kandiah, T. 'The Transformational Challenge and the Teacher of English', in *Language Learning* 20, 1970, 151–182.

König, Ekkehard. 'Transformational Grammar and Contrastive Analysis', in *PAKS-Arbeitsbericht* 6, Stuttgart, 1970, 43–57.

Krohn, Robert. 'The Role of Linguistics in TEFL Methodology', in *Language Learning* 20, 1970, 103–108.

Kuentz, Pierre. 'La linguistique moderne et l'enseignement du français', in *Le français d'aujourd'hui* 2, 1968, 6–9.

Kufner, Herbert L. 'Lerntheorie, Linguistik und Sprachunterricht', in *Probleme der kontrastiven Grammatik*, Düsseldorf, Pädagogischer Verlag Schwann, 1970, 160–174.

Lado, Robert. *Linguistics across Cultures*, Ann Arbor, The University of Michigan Press, 1957.

Lakoff, Robin. 'Transformational Grammar and Language Teaching', in *Language Learning* 19, 1969, 117–140.

Lambert, Wallace E. 'Psychological Approaches to the Study of Language', in *Modern Language Journal* 47, 1963, 114–121.

Lambert, W. E., Gardner, R. C., Olton, R. and Tunstall, K. 'A Study of the Roles of Attitudes and Motivation in Second-Language Learning', in Fishman, J. A. *Readings in the Sociology of Language*, The Hague, Mouton, 1968, 473–491.

Lamberts, J. J. 'Basic Concepts for Teaching from Structural Linguistics', in *The English Journal* 49/3, 1960, 172–176.

Lamendella, John T. 'Review of W. E. Rutherford, *Modern English*', in *Language Learning* 19, 1969, 147–160.

Lamendella, John T. 'On the irrelevance of Transformational Grammar to Language Pedagogy,' in *Language Learning* 19, 1969, 255–270.

Lechler, Hans-Joachim. 'Vom Substitution Table zur Composition, Wege zum sicheren Schreiben im Englischen', in *Der fremdsprachliche Unterricht* **4**, 1967, 70–78.

Léon, Pierre R. *Prononciation du français standard. Aide-mémoire d'orthoépie*, Paris, Didier, 1966.

Léon, Pierre R. *Laboratoire de langues et correction phonétique*, Paris, Didier, 1962.

Léon, Monique. *Exercices systématiques de prononciation française*, Paris, Hachette/Larousse, 1964.

Lester, Mark (ed.). *Readings in Applied Transformational Grammar*, New York, Holt, Rinehart and Winston, 1970.

Lester, Mark. 'The Value of Transformational Grammar in Teaching Composition', in *College Composition and Communication* **18**, 1967, 227–231; reprinted in *Readings in Applied Transformational Grammar*, New York, Holt, Rinehart and Winston, 1970, 201–209.

Levin, Samuel R. 'Comparing Traditional and Structural Grammar', in *College English* **21**, 1960, 260–265; reprinted in Allen, H. B., *Readings in Applied English Linguistics*, New York, Appleton-Century-Crofts, 2nd ed., 1964, 46–53.

Linguistik und Pädagogik I, *Sprache im technischen Zeitalter* **32**, 1969.

Linguistik und Pädagogik II, *Sprache im technischen Zeitalter* **33**, 1970.

Long, Ralph B. Linguistic Universals, Deep Structure and English as a Second Language, Paper given at the Third Annual TESOL Convention, Chicago, 1969.

Lukenbill, Jeffrey. 'Classroom Grammarians', in *The English Journal* **54**, 1965, 227–230, 237.

Lyons, John and Wales, R. J. *Psycholinguistics Papers*, Edinburgh University Press, 1966.

Mackey, W. F. 'Applied Linguistics, Its Meaning and Use', in *Journal of English Teaching* **1/3**, 1968, 6–16.

McNeill, D. 'Developmental Psycholinguistics', in Smith, F. and Miller, G. A. *The Genesis of Language*, Cambridge, MIT Press, 1966, 15–84.

Meyer, Hans-Lothar. 'Zur Anwendung der Transformationsgrammatik im Englischunterricht', in *Linguistik und Didaktik* **2**, 1970, 137–154.

Meys, W. J. 'De transformationele theorie en het vreemdetalenonderwijs', in *Levende Talen* **254**, 1969, 10–22.

Mildenberger, Kenneth W. 'Confusing Signposts—The Relevance of Applied Linguistics', in *Monograph Series on Languages and Linguistics* **21**, 1968, 205–213.

Molina, Hubert. 'Transformational Grammar in Teaching Spanish', in *Hispania* **51/2**, 1968, 284–286.

Moreno, P. 'Bases de una «grammatica pedagogica» para la ensenanza de los idiomos extranjeros', in *Revista di linguistica aplicada* **6**, 1968, 10–19.

Motsch, Wolfgang. 'Sprachwissenschaft und Sprachunterricht', in *Deutsch als Fremdsprache* **1–2**, 1970, 17–25.

Moulton, William G. 'Linguistics and Language Teaching in the United States, 1940–1960', in *Trends in European and American Linguistics*, Utrecht, 1962, 82–109.

Moulton, William G. 'What is Structural Drill?' in Gravit, F. W. and

Valdman, Albert, *Structural Drill and the Language Laboratory*, Bloomington, Indiana University, 1963, 3–15.

Muller, Gert. 'Sprachunterricht und Sprachwissenschaft', in *Der fremdsprachliche Unterricht* 3, 1967, 2–11.

Muskat-Tabokowska, E. 'The Notions of Performance and Competence in Language Teaching', in *Language Learning* 19, 1969, 41–54.

Newmark, Leonard. 'Grammatical Theory and the Teaching of English as a Second Language', in Lester, Mark, *Readings in Applied Transformational Grammar*, New York, Holt, Rinehart and Winston, 1970, 210–218.

Newmark, Leonard. 'How not to Interfere with Language Learning', in *IJAL* 32, 1966, 77–83; reprinted in Lester, Mark, *Readings in Applied Transformational Grammar*, New York, Holt, Rinehart and Winston, 1970, 219–227.

Newmark, Leonard and Reibel, David A. 'Necessity and Sufficiency in Language Learning', in *IRAL* 6, 1968, 145–161; reprinted in Lester, Mark, *Readings in Applied Transformational Grammar*, New York, Holt, Rinehart and Winston, 1970, 228–252.

Newsome, Verna L. 'Expansions and Transformations to Improve Sentences', in *The English Journal* 53, 1964, 327–335.

Ney, James W. 'Transformation Grammar in the Ryudai Classroom', in *Language Learning* 15, 1965, 51–59.

Nickel, Gerhard. 'Angewandte Sprachwissenschaft und Fremdsprachenunterricht', in *Die deutsche Schule*, 1968, 218 ff.

Nickel, Gerhard. 'Contrastive Linguistics and Language Teaching', in *Papers in Contrastive Linguistics*, London, Cambridge University Press, 1971.

Nickel, Gerhard. 'Welche Grammatik für den Fremdsprachenunterricht?' in *Praxis des neusprachlichen Unterrichts* 14, 1967, 1 ff.

Nickel, Gerhard and Wagner, Karl-Heinz. 'Contrastive Linguistics and Language Teaching', in *IRAL* 6, 1968, 233–255.

Nietz, John A. 'Old Secondary School Grammar Textbooks', in *The English Journal* 54, 1965, 541–546.

O'Donnell, W. R. 'The Teaching of Grammar', in Fraser, H. and O'Donnell, W. R., *Applied Linguistics and the Teaching of English*, London, Longman, 1973 (2nd ed.), 159–175.

Ohmann, Richard. 'Generative Grammars and the Concept of Literary Style', in *Word* 20, 1964, 423–439; reprinted in Lester, Mark, *Readings in Applied Transformational Grammar*, New York, Holt, Rinehart and Winston, 1970, 117–136.

Ohmann, Richard. 'Literature as Sentences', in *College English* 27, 1966, 261–267; reprinted in Lester, Mark, *Readings in Applied Transformational Grammar*, New York, Holt, Rinehart and Winston, 1970, 137–148.

Oller, Jr., J. W. 'Transformational Theory and Pragmatics', in *Modern Language Journal* 54, 1970, 504–507.

O'Neil, Wayne A. *Kernels and Transformations, A Modern Grammar of English*, New York, McGraw-Hill, 1965.

Palmer, Harold E. *The Principles of Language Study*, London, Harrap, 1922, (new ed.) Oxford University Press, 1964.

Peizer, D. B. and Olmsted, D. L. *Modules of Grammar Acquisition*, in *Language* **45**, 1969, 60–96.

Peytard, J. and Genouvrier, E. *Linguistique et enseignement du français*, Paris, Larousse, 1970.

Pfister, Raimund. 'Thesen zu Linguistik und Sprachunterricht', in *Linguistische Berichte* **7**, 1970, 71–73.

Pincas, Anita. ' "Transformational", "Generative", and the EFL Teacher', in *English Language Teaching* **22**, 1968, 210–220.

Politzer, Robert L. *Teaching French, An Introduction to Applied Linguistics*, New York, Blaisdell, 1960.

Politzer, Robert L. 'The Impact of Linguistics on Language Teaching: Past, Present and Future', in *Modern Language Journal* **48**, 1964.

Premier colloque canadien de linguistique appliquée, Ottawa, University, 1969.

Ritchie, William C. 'Some Implications of Generative Grammar for the Construction of Courses in English as a Foreign Language', in *Language Learning* **17**, 1967, 45–69, 111–131.

Rivers, Wilga M. 'Contrastive Linguistics in Textbook and Classroom', in *Monograph Series on Languages and Linguistics* **21**, 1968, 151–158.

Rivers, Wilga M. *Teaching Foreign-Language Skills*, Chicago, University Press, 1968.

Rivers, Wilga M. *The Psychologist and the Foreign-language Teacher*, Chicago, University Press, 1964.

Roberts, Paul, Foreword, in Wilson, G. *A Linguistics Reader*, New York, Harper and Row, 1967, ix–xxix.

Roberts, Paul. 'The Relation of Linguistics to the Teaching of English', in *College English* **22**, 1960, 1–9; reprinted in Wilson, G. *A Linguistics Reader*, New York, Harper and Row, 1967, 27–37.

Rojas, Colette. 'L'enseignement de la grammaire', in *Le français dans le monde* **65**, 1969, 50–57.

Rosenbaum, Peter S. 'On the Role of Linguistics in the Teaching of English', in *Harvard Educational Review* **35**, 1965, 322–348; reprinted in Reibel, D. A. and Schane, S. A., *Modern Studies in English, Readings in Transformational Grammar*, Englewood Cliffs, Prentice-Hall, 1969, 467–481.

Ross, Janet. 'Controlled Writing, A Transformational Approach', in *TESOL Quarterly* **2/4**, 1968, 253–261.

Roth, E. 'Die Transformationsgrammatik im Englischunterricht', in *Die neueren Sprachen* **68**, 1969, 313–322.

Rothschild, Thomas. 'Linguistik in der Schule, Zur Diskussion einer Reform des Deutsch-Unterrichts', in *Sprache im technischen Zeitalter* **33**, 1970, 34–44.

Roulet, E. 'Vers une grammaire de l'emploi et de l'apprentissage de la langue', in *Proceedings of the Third International Congress of Applied Linguistics*, Heidelberg, Julius Groos, 1973.

Roulet, E. 'L'élaboration de matériel didactique pour l'enseignement des langues maternelle et secondes: leçons de la linguistique appliquée', in *Bulletin CILA* **18**, 1973.

Roulet, E. 'Quelques grammaires utiles à l'élaboration d'exercices structuraux pour le laboratoire de langues', in *Bulletin CILA* **4**, 1967, 4–20.

Roulet, E. *Les modèles de grammaire et leurs applications à l'enseigne-ment des langues vivantes*; English translation: *Grammatical Models and their Application in the Teaching of Modern Languages*, Strasbourg, Conseil de l'Europe 1970, mimeo; French translation, reprinted in *Revue des langues vivantes* **37**, 1971, 582–604 and *Le français dans le monde* **85**, 1971, 6–15; English translation reprinted in *Contact* **18–19**, 1972, 21–35.

Rutherford, W. E. 'Deep and Surface Structure, and the Language Drill', in *TESOL Quarterly* **2/2** 1968, 71–79.

Saporta, S. 'Applied Linguistics and Generative Grammar', in Valdman, A., *Trends in Modern Language Teaching*, New York, McGraw-Hill, 1966, 81–92.

Schap, Keith. 'Pronoun Stress and the Composition Teacher', in *Language Learning* **16**, 1966, 161–172.

Scott, Charles T. 'The Linguistic Basis for the Development of Reading Skill', in *Modern Language Journal* **50**, 1966, 535–544.

Scott, Charles T. 'Transformational Theory and English as a Second Language/Dialect', in *Monograph Series on Languages and Linguistics* **22**, 1969, 75–86.

Slama-Cazacu, Tatiana. 'La linguistique appliquée et quelques problèmes psycholinguistiques de l'enseignement des langues', in *Cahiers de linguis-tique théorique et appliquée* **5**, 1968, 221–246.

Sledd, James. 'Grammar or Grammarye?', in *The English Journal* **49/5**, 1960, 293–303; reprinted in Wilson, G., *A Linguistics Reader*, New York, Harper and Row, 1967, 125–135.

Smith, Philip D. *A Comparison of the Cognitive and Audio-lingual Ap-proaches to Foreign-Language Instruction* (*The Pennsylvania Foreign Language Project*), Philadelphia, Center for Curriculum Development, 1970.

Sowinski, Bernhard. 'Möglichkeiten und Grenzen strukturalistischer Sprachbetrachtung in der Schule', in *Wirkendes Wort* **3**, 1969, 163–175.

Spolsky, Bernard. 'Computer-based Instruction and the Criteria for Pedagogical Grammars', in *Language Learning* **15**, 1965, 137–145.

Spolsky, Bernard. 'Linguistics and Language Pedagogy—Applications or Implications?' in *Monograph Series on Languages and Linguistics* **22**, 1969, 143–155.

Stalb, Heinrich. 'Versuche und Anregungen zur Arbeit mit der generativen Grammatik auf der Oberstufe', in *Linguistik und Didaktik* **5**, 1971, 1–23.

Steiner, Florence. 'The Role of Applied Linguistics in the Teaching of Spanish and French', in *Illinois Journal of Education* **58/6**, 1966, 7–10.

Stern, H. H. *Grammar in Language Teaching*, mimeo, unpublished.

Stern, H. H. 'The Issues and Directions of Language Learning', in *Canadian Modern Language Review* **27/1**, 1970, 47–50.

Strevens, Peter. 'Two Ways of Looking at Error-Analysis', in *Zielsprache Deutsch* **1**, 1971, 1–6.

Stryker, Shirley L. 'Applied Linguistics: Principles and Techniques', in *English Teaching Forum* **7/5**, 1969.

Thomas, Owen. 'Generative Grammar: Toward Unification and Simplification', in *The English Journal* **51**, 1962, 94–99; reprinted in Allen H. B., *Readings in Applied English Linguistics*, New York, Appleton-Century-Crofts (2nd ed.), 1964, 405–414.

Thomas, Owen. *Transformational Grammar and the Teacher of English*, New York, Holt, Rinehart and Winston, 1965.

Thorne, J. P. 'Generative Grammar and Stylistic Analysis', in Lyons, John, *New Horizons in Linguistics*, Harmondsworth, Penguin Books, 1970, 185–197.

Thorne, J. P. 'Stylistics and Generative Grammar', in *Journal of Linguistics* **1/1**, 1965.

Titone, Renzo. 'Linee per una sperimentazione sulla didattica della grammatica', in *Homo loquens* **1**, 1968, 3–14.

Valdman, Albert. 'Norme pédagogique: les structures interrogatives du français', in *IRAL* **5**, 1967, 3–10.

Valdman, Albert. *Applied Linguistics: French, A Guide for Teachers*, Boston, D.C. Heath and Co., 1961.

Viereck, Wolfgang. 'Die Revolution in der Grammatik und das amerikanische Schulbuch', in *Praxis des neusprachlichen Unterrichts* **16**, 1969, 55–68.

Vinay, Jean-Paul. 'Enseignement et apprentissage d'une seconde langue', in Martinet, A. (ed.), *Le Langage*, Paris, Gallimard, 1968, 685–728.

Wagner, Karl-Heinz. 'Probleme der kontrastiven Sprachwissenschaft', in *Sprache im technischen Zeitalter* **32**, 1969, 305–326.

Wagner, Karl-Heinz. 'The Relevance of the Notion "Deep Structure" to Contrastive Analysis', in *PAKS-Arbeitsbericht* **6**, Stuttgart, 1970, 1–42.

Wagner, R. L. 'A propos de grammaires: éloges, critiques, aveux', in *Le français dans le monde* **40**, 1966, 14–22.

Walmsley, J. B. 'Transformational Theory and Translation', in *IRAL* **8**, 1970, 185–199.

Wardhaugh, Ronald. 'If Grammar, which Grammar, and How?' in *College English* **29/4**, 1968, 303–309.

Wardhaugh, Ronald. *Reading: A Linguistic Perspective*, New York, Harcourt, Brace and World, 1969.

Wardhaugh, Ronald. 'Some Current Problems in Second-Language Teaching', in *Language Learning* **17**, 1967, 21–26.

Wardhaugh, Ronald. 'Three Approaches to Contrastive Phonological Analysis', in *Canadian Journal of Linguistics* **13/1**, 1967, 3–14.

Weber, H. 'Einige Gedanken zu den linguistischen Grundlagen des Fremdsprachenunterrichts', in *Bulletin CILA* **11**, 1970, 18–32.

Widdowson, H. G. 'Directions in the Teaching of Discourse', in Corder, S. P. and Roulet, E. (eds.). *Theoretical Linguistic Models in Applied Linguistics*, Brussels, AIMAV and Paris, Didier, 1973.

Wisser, B. 'Die Rolle der Grammatik im Englischunterricht', in *Die neueren Sprachen* **67**, 1968, 132–140.

Wunderlich, Dieter. 'Unterrichten als Dialog', in *Sprache im technischen Zeitalter* **32**, 1969, 263–287.

Wyatt, James L. 'The Common-Core Transformational Grammar: A

Contrastive Model', in *Journal of English as a Second Language* **2/2**, 1967, 51–65.

Wyler, Siegfried. 'Generativ-transformationelle Grammatik und Schul-Grammatik', in *Bulletin CILA* **11**, 1970, 33–51.

Wyler, Siegfried. 'Zur Integration der strukturellen Grammatik in den traditionellen Unterricht', in *Der fremdsprachliche Unterricht* **3**, 1967, 12–21.

Zeller, Hella. 'Transformationsgrammatik und Sprachunterricht', in *Angewandte Linguistik—Französisch*, Kiel, Arbeitsgruppe Angewandte Linguistik: Französisch, 1970, 89–102.

Zidonis, Frank J. 'Generative Grammar: A Report on Research', in *The English Journal* **54**, 1965, 405–409.

C. Language teaching coursebooks

Abbs, Brian, Cook, Vivian and Underwood, Mary. *Realistic English*, London, Oxford University Press, 1968.

Bloomfield, Leonard and Barnhart, C. L. *Let's Read, A Linguistic Approach*, Detroit, Wayne State University Press, 1961.

Chevalier, Jean-Claude, Blanche-Benveniste, C., Arrivé, M. and Peytard, J. *Grammaire Larousse du français contemporain*, Paris, Larousse, 1964.

Croft, K. *English Noun Compounds*, Washington, Georgetown University 1964.

Delattre, Pierre. *Principes de phonétique française à l'usage des étudiants anglo-américains*, Middlebury (Vermont), Summer School in French (2nd ed.)., 1951.

Dickinson, Leslie and Mackin, Ronald. *Varieties of Spoken English*, London, Oxford University Press, 1969.

Dostert, Leon. *Spoken French, Basic Course*, Washington, Georgetown, University Press (2nd ed.) 1956.

Eschliman, H. R., Jones, R. C., Burkett, T. R. *Generative English Handbook*, Belmont (Calif.), Wadsworth Publishing Co. 1968.

French, F. G. *English in Tables*, London, Oxford University Press, 1960.

Fries, Charles C. *American-English Grammar, The Grammatical Structures of Present-Day American English with Special References to Social Differences or Class Dialects*, New York, Appleton-Century, 1940.

George, H. V. *101 Substitution Tables for Students of English*, Cambridge, University Press, 1967.

Gerighausen, J. and Martin, H. *L'allemand tel qu'on le parle*, Heidelberg, Julius Groos, 1968.

Grévisse, Maurice. *Précis de grammaire française*, Gembloux, Duculot (26th ed.).

Hornby, A. S. *A Guide to Patterns and Usage in English*, London, Oxford University Press, 1954.

Lado, Robert and Fries, Charles C. *English Sentence Patterns*, Ann Arbor, (7th ed.). 1962.

Malzac, Jacques. *Grammaire nouvelle*, Paris, Gamma, 1970.

Martinet, A. *Initiation pratique à l'anglais*, Lyon, IAC, 1947.

Marty, Ferdinand. *Spoken and Written French for the Language Laboratory*, Wellesley, Audio-Visual Publications (2nd ed.), 1958.

Mauger, G. *Grammaire pratique du français d'aujourd'hui, langue parlée, langue écrite*, Paris, Hachette, 1968.

Meuron, Luc de and Bron, Claude. *Grammaire française*, Neuchâtel, Messeiller (5th ed.), 1962.

Mueller, T. H., Mayer, E. N. and Niedzielski, H. *Handbook of French Structure*, New York, Harcourt, Brace and World, 1968.

Nilsen, Don L. F. and A. P. *A Transformational Approach to Composition*, Kabul University, 1969, mimeo.

Rand, Earl. *Constructing Dialogs*, New York, Holt, Rinehart and Winston, 1969.

Richard, P. M. and Hall, Wendy. *Anglais seconde langue, classe de 4e*, Paris, Hachette, 1960.

Roberts, Paul. *English Sentences*, New York, Harcourt, Brace and World, 1962.

Roberts, Paul. *English Syntax, Alternate Edition, A Programed Introduction to Transformational Grammar*, New York, Harcourt, Brace and World, 1964.

Roberts, Paul. *Patterns of English*, New York, Harcourt, Brace and World, 1956.

Roberts, Paul. *The Roberts English Series, A Linguistic Program*, New York, Harcourt, Brace and World, 1966.

Roberts, Paul. *Understanding Grammar*, New York, Harper and Row, 1964.

Rutherford, William E. *Modern English, A Textbook for Foreign Students*, New York, Harcourt, Brace and World, 1968.

Schaap, E. *English Grammar and Noun Idioms for Foreigners*, London. McMillan (2nd ed.), rev. 1960.

Schwab, William. *Guide to Modern Grammar and Exposition*, New York, Harper and Row, 1967.

Voix et images de France, Paris, Didier, s.d.

Zandvoort, R. W. *Grammaire descriptive de l'anglais contemporain*, Lyon, IAC, 1949.